D1111002

"Come!" says the abortion culture, "Be reasonable, debate us, write pamphlets, preach fine sermons, have a symbolic march or two, or even do a Rescue once if you have to; but be respectable. Don't actually live as if you believe the unborn are living human beings. Be honest. Whatever you might say in your sermons, you know that when the judge says, 'Stop acting like Christ!' you'll stop."

— *The World*

You were bought at a price. Therefore glorify God in your body and in your spirit, which are God's.

— *The Apostle*

SHATTERING
THE
DARKNESS

The Crisis of the Cross
in the Church Today

SHATTERING
THE
DARKNESS

The Crisis of the Cross
in the Church Today

By JOSEPH LAPSLEY FOREMAN

Preface by

RUTH BELL GRAHAM

Foreword by

GEORGE GRANT

THE COOLING SPRING PRESS
Montreat

Published by The Cooling Spring Press
A Division of Challenge House
313 Georgia Terrace
Montreat, North Carolina 28757

Manufactured in the United States of America

Cover Design by Chris West

Diagrams by Mark Lucas

Copyright © 1992 by Joseph L. Foreman

Library of Congress Cataloging-in-Publication Data:

Foreman, Joseph Lapsley, 1954-
       Shattering the darkness : the crisis of the cross in the church
today / Joseph Lapsley Foreman ; preface by Ruth Bell Graham
; foreword by George Grant.
              p.   cm.
       1. Abortion--Religious aspects--Christianity.   2. Pro-life
movement--United States.   3. Operation Rescue (Organization)
4. Government, Resistance to--Religious aspects--Christianity.
5. Government, Resistance to--United States.   6. Holy Cross.
7. Christianity and social problems--United States.   8. United
States--Politics and government--1989-   I. Title.
HQ767.25.F67   1992
261.8'36667'0973--dc20   92-52941

ISBN 0-935883-03-7 (pbk.) : $9.95

DEDICATED TO RANDALL TERRY AND JOAN ANDREWS BELL

This book, like any good thing in the pro-life movement after 1988, is dedicated to these two whose relentless vision and energy made it possible. Without their personal work, sacrifice, and dedication in two very different arenas, there would be no new generation of pro-life leadership emerging today — and the impact of the main-line leadership would be considerably lessened. It was Joan's uncompromising two-and-a-half years of solitary confinement in prison which forced us all to realize that each child is a real person *worth* any level of sacrifice to protect, and it was Randy who made the idea of sacrifice reasonable and even popular again in the American Church. It is not too much to say that anyone who has begun to support himself in any sort of full time pro-life work after 1988 is in debt to Randy and should publicly recognize his work and thank him for it. We are all working out of the vision which Joan and Randy made real. Without what they did we would be like little candles on a glacier going out one by one, instead of where we are today: realistically planning how we can unite in a blaze which will destroy every vestige of legalized child murder. They kicked free a fifteen-year logjam and we've been rumbling down the mountain ever since, flying on the wings of a gathering storm.

ACKNOWLEDGEMENTS

As this manuscript evolved over the last five years, many people have read its drafts and encouraged me to keep at it. Susan Odom has been chief among these. Many drafts were written and typed and corrected by mail from jail, thanks to Jan Opris who freed Bonnie to type for me, and to Martha Turner and Sue Yingst. The editors at Cooling Spring have given me most helpful and penetrating criticisms over the years. And thanks to Anna Marie Davis, Sue Yingst, and Beth Crawford who did the galley proofs.

Few of the ideas set out here are original with me. I must thank Jack and Pat O'Brien and Tom Herlihy for being great role-models; Doug and Owenna Nagy for introducing me to Rescue; Richard Cowden-Guido for always being game for an argument; Pastor John Brown of Atlanta for his insight on God's wonderful plan for His people in America; Dan and Melissa Duffy for their brutal honesty; Police officer Chet Gallagher for warning me about worshipping Baal Law-and-Order; and, not least, the LBC who spent hours thrashing out a whole spectrum of ideas in order to come up with those which would actually enable Operation Rescue to fly.

I also thank Mike McMonagle for his friendship, counsel, and for taking me to Operation Rescue's first organizing meeting; and Bryan Brown, Richard Cash, Philip and Becky Elder, and Eva Edl for vital encouragement at crucial points in the production of this book.

My thanks are especially due to the Missionaries who have permitted me the time away from my commitment to rescue daily, so that I could finish this book — Bob Roethlisberger, Ron Brock, Bryan Longworth, Gary, Melody and Caleb McCullough, Louise and Bruce Carper, JoAnna Luttrell, Anne Franczek, Eva Edl, Matt Trewhella, Joe Washburn — and all the other Missionaries. These people, like my wife, Anne, pay in their lives for what I speak of so freely here.

And I am grateful to my children, Laurel, Jeremy, Joshua, Rachel, and Zachary, for their patience. I pray that they, with their children's children and yours, who will be here long after we are gone, will be equipped by our example to be faithful in the world which you and I leave to them.

SHATTERING THE DARKNESS

Table of Contents

PREFACE BY RUTH BELL GRAHAM

In this compelling book Joseph Foreman outlines the path which God has set before him. Not all will be called to follow his exact path, but the issues he raises cannot be dodged if we are to be faithful to our calling to be light and salt in the world. If at times his voice raises blisters, perhaps it is because he has seen more clearly than most the terrible price of indifference and compromise.

I have known Joseph Foreman since he was a boy growing up in the congregation where I also am a member. Now with thousands across the land I am thankful for his commitment and his life.

Little Piney Cove
Montreat, North Carolina
March, 1992

FOREWORD BY GEORGE GRANT

"Murder is not debatable."

Those words were uttered in July of 1917 by Theodore Roosevelt. True then, they are just as certainly true today.

Responding to a prominent citizen's public defense of a white mob's murder of defenseless black citizens in East St. Louis, he said:

> Justice is not merely words. It is to be translated into living acts . . . . Shall we by silence acquiesce in this amazing apology for the murder of men, women and children in our own country?
>
> Never will I sit motionless while directly or indirectly apology is made for the murder of the helpless.
>
> . . . .
>
> We hope to advance throughout the world the peace of righteousness and brotherhood; surely we can best do so when we insist upon this peace of righteousness and brotherhood within our own borders.
>
> In securing such a peace the first essential is to guarantee to every man the most elementary of rights, the right to his own life. Murder is not debatable.[1]

There are those who would have us believe that abortion — that flagrant child-killing on demand — is a debatable issue today. But murder is not debatable.

They would have us believe that because the procedures are sanitized in our hospitals, subsidized by our taxes, and lionized by the media, that abortion is somehow legitimate. But, murder is not debatable.

They would have us fall for their verbal trifles and tricks; to accept their twisted logic that somehow killing a living baby in its mother's womb is merely a personal choice, a material right, a reproductive freedom, or a matter between a woman and

---

[1] *The Foes of Our Own Household*. New York: George H. Doran Company, 1917, pages 280-281, and 286.

her doctor. But murder is not debatable.

Sadly, that kind of fierce conviction so ably displayed by men like Roosevelt has somehow been lost in the current rhetoric of abortion politics. Questions about methodology or tactics or strategies or personalities have begun to supersede any other consideration — even within the Christian community. As a result, this epic struggle for truth, justice, and mercy has generated far more heat than light.

Until now.

Joseph Foreman, for years a respected and courageous Rescue leader, has upped the spiritual and intellectual ante with this incisive and original book. Like Roosevelt before him, he has served up large portions of both heat and light — a much needed corrective in view of the fact that indeed, murder is not debatable.

Be assured that this is not a book which is likely to satisfy your mind completely. It does not offer pat answers to all your plaguing questions about the pro-life movement in general or about Rescue in particular. But then that was never Joseph's intention. To offer pat answers is merely to smother authenticity. To satisfy a mind completely may be merely to stop it from thinking. To disturb a mind — to stimulate it, to provoke it, to inspire it, and then to motivate it — is the job of any authentic argument or any good book. Joseph does that job, and he does it well.

Instead of defending the methodology of Rescue, he defines it; instead of pleading the cause of Rescue, he pronounces it; and his definitions and pronouncements are all conceived in terms of the practical implications of the Cross of Christ. That is a powerful conception — one which could well shake the already shaky foundations of the modern church.

You may disagree with Joseph Foreman. You may even disparage him. But one thing is certain: you simply cannot dismiss him. He raises questions which have too long been ignored — central questions about the nature of faith, the character of God, the standard of faithfulness, the function of the priesthood of believers, the relevance of martyrdom, and the split between rhetoric and reality. The fact is, Joseph Foreman's

Biblically argued conception of the work, witness, and way of the Cross — as well as his dramatic missionary response to that work, witness, and way — may well be the most significant theological development in the pro-life movement in recent days.

In this book you'll see why. It is as prophetic and passionate as you might expect. But it is also carefully reasoned from the perspective of a Reformed catholicity which is an all too rare attribute in pro-life circles — in fact, it is an all too rare attribute in any circle. It is sure to make you think. And squirm.

Thus, I heartily recommend *Shattering the Darkness*. It is a book which warrants a serious and substantive hearing.

It is a book which warrants decisive and faithful action.

Theodore Roosevelt was right: Murder is not debatable.

George Grant

Legacy Communications
Franklin, Tennessee
March, 1992

REFLECTION BY GARY DEMAR

East German border guard Ingo Heinrich killed a man escaping East Berlin for the freedom in the West. He justified his action by saying, "I was just following orders to shoot to kill." In the eyes of his supervisors, Heinrich's actions were not only legal, they were commendable. But Heinrich now lives in a *new* Berlin, serving 3 1/2 years in prison. Judge Theodore Seidel ruled that he was guilty of following the laws of his country rather than his conscience: "Not everything that is legal is right."

The principle that an individual is bound by a higher moral authority, beyond what civil sanctioned laws provide, was established in West Germany decades ago, during the trials of Nazi war criminals.

Freedom-loving Americans applauded the ruling. But is the abortion issue any different? Abortion is legal, but in Biblical terms it is not right. Why doesn't America applaud those who seek to rescue the preborn from the border guards of the abortion industry? Why doesn't Seidel's "Not everything that is legal is right!" thunder through the churches of America?

Yes, the churches of America! Operation Rescue is not only an indictment of Congress, the courts, and the abortionists, it is first and foremost an indictment of the Christian church. Most Christians refuse to stand against abortion, so dedicated groups of believers have chosen to stand, sit, and kneel in front of the entrances to abortuaries. For this they are condemned. Are their efforts different from guards who chose not to follow East German law by purposely firing wide or not firing at all?

In *Shattering the Darkness,* Joseph Foreman has extended the argument and answered the question. In the final analysis, all Christians must be persuaded with *Biblical* arguments. Not even the conscience is a good enough ethical guide. If you fear having your mind changed, or even challenged, then do not read *Shattering the Darkness.*

American Vision
Atlanta, Georgia
March, 1992

AUTHOR'S INTRODUCTION:

THE CRISIS OF THE CROSS

Our goal is to make it as safe, legal, and normal to protect the innocent from murder as it is now safe, legal, and normal to kill them. The issue is not whether abortion or euthanasia should be illegal, but whether Christians should ever make what men call "legal" the limit of what they do to love their neighbor. More than any other single factor, the extent to which we obey God will determine what is and is not legal for generations. Every generation faces the crisis of the Cross: Can we love God with all our being and love our neighbor as ourselves? This is the issue of Christianity and Civilization. This is Rescue.

How can we become a light which will not just illumine, but will shatter the darkness? This has been the cultural question of God's people throughout the ages. It is in this tradition that Operation Rescue stands.

With the taming of Rescue as a movement, the voice of the children, crying out through the lives put on the line for them, has been briefly muffled. But not all the seed fell on thorny ground. There are hundreds of thousands of Christians in whose hearts it is beginning to grow. It will bear fruit in time. Satan's challenge to the name of God will not go away on its own, and can only lead to the flowering or withering of the Church. If Wichita's 1991 Summer of Mercy is a foretaste, next time there will be tens of thousands in the streets. Will we remain non-violent? Will we be satisfied to just kick our country's hinder parts? Or will we touch the nation's heart? I believe we can touch hearts if we will learn the lessons of Operation Rescue.

Shattering the Darkness is the heart of what the Rescue Movement is all about — taking up the Cross of our Lord. It could just as easily be a book about world missions, inner city ministry, Christian businessmen, or the Christian marriage and home. The material would not change significantly, because the same Cross of Jesus Christ which shatters the dark of abortion shatters the darkness that hinders all walks of the Christian life. The spiritual journey of this movement sheds a burning light on the challenge of what it means to be a Christian in all we do.

This book can help you see your whole life as a mission commissioned by God. I do not want to recruit you to some organization. God requires much more and the hour is late for our generation. No, I want to help you transform even the way you wash dishes, whether you ever sit-in at an abortion clinic or not. Discover the thousands of years of Rescue history which stand behind us — not in a history lesson, but in the simple orthodox doctrines we pass on to our children from their earliest years: the doctrines of creation, providence, the atonement, and the incarnation; God is three and He is One; God created everything good; we are sinners; God punishes sin; Jesus loves you; God is in control and has a plan for your life; Jesus is God become man, so God could punish Jesus and save you; God through Jesus will make everything clean and new; Jesus wants you to obey Him; Jesus wants you to be like Him; God will provide for you in everything when you obey and act like Him. Kids, now that you've learned your Sunday school lesson, who wants to tell God you're sorry and from now on you want to obey and be like Jesus?

These are such simple doctrines that we forget how they transform not only the lives of anyone who takes them seriously, but whole societies of those who have taken them seriously. Who wants Jesus in his heart? . . . Well, the more I learn about this Jesus, the more I realize that He is not very likable. Frankly, I like much better the positive public image portrayed by a successful conference speaker, evangelist, missionary, or Christian businessman! I would much rather be nicer than Jesus. This Jesus of Sunday school and the Scriptures is dangerous. I am very uncomfortable with the Jesus who rescued me, coming into my heart — the Jesus of Matthew 23 and 25, of Revelation 2 and 3, who stands in righteous anger at the door of the Church, His Church, knocking. He is not very nice. He insists that we either open to Him, or He destroys that door, our house with it, seizes His candlestick, snuffs out our light, and goes away.

When you start taking these Sunday school doctrines seriously, you find that the heart of authentic Christianity is Rescue. Not the act of sitting-in at abortion clinics, not a complex systematic theology, but the heart of utter abandonment

to God on behalf of others, regardless of risk and price —
something even a small child understands. It is this heart I want
you to see, because it is God's heart — His Son's Cross.

When we learn to die to self, then giving ourselves to
Rescue others will seem quite normal — neither heroic, nor
radical, nor wrong. If reading this book does not get you
arrested, that is fine, if only you understand the way of the
Cross for what God has called *you* to do. The problem is not
that we do *not* want to leave everything and follow Jesus. In
some sense we *do* want to. We sing about it in most of our
hymns. We read about it in our Bibles and missionary books.
The simplest formulas of our faith assume it. But for most it is
an idle dream — we could not lose our lives in order to find
them even if we tried. That is the tragedy which Operation
Rescue merely uncovered in the Church — and we resent Rescue
for it. It showed us how we could not even cross the street to
save a baby, much less be bold in witness to our neighbors, or
tithe, or deal with pornography, or keep our churches from
splitting over hairs, or get out of debt, or even lower our
personal life-styles a notch so as to enable others to do more
work in the kingdom. The fact is, America, we do not want to
put ourselves in a position where, for God's victory we must die
to our own agendas. Dying to self has become merely an
internal, existential experience which makes us feel at peace in
our little hearts. It has been made exciting by listening to the
right television preachers and schools of church growth.

It was into this exciting world of Spiritual Warfare
American Style that Operation Rescue came with a beautifully
tailored program: Die to yourself on the weekend and still make
it to work on Monday (or Tuesday) morning. We became
popular because all Christians know the undeniable urgency of
dying to ourselves, obeying God, and saving a baby's life.
Operation Rescue showed us how we could sacrifice like a hero
in a way which fits a busy schedule. It was like not having to
win the Congressional Medal of Honor posthumously. You can
see both why we succeeded, as well as why, sooner or later, the
first push would have to run out of gas.

The early successes in the 1988 Siege of Atlanta, and then
in the 1991 Summer of Mercy in Wichita, showed that it is easy

to make child-killing physically impossible and unpopular. *Any city large enough to sport a child-killing doctor has more than enough Christians to make him stop killing and to keep the legal system from persecuting the Christians who stop the killing.* But the story of Operation Rescue in these two cities also showed how ill prepared we were to face up to a world determined to protect legalized murder. At the first sign of resistance we melted and began to turn to the political doors which had crept open a few inches because of our boldness. It was as if we wanted political coercion to suffice where our willingness to take up our cross would cost us too much. *We still thought of Rescue as "street level coercion" instead of laying down our lives.* When the activist coercion fails, we turn to political coercion, and when we think political coercion is not working, we try activist coercion. But God is looking for so much more. He is not looking for a people who will travel land and sea to discover the most efficient way to maximize other people's burdens while minimizing their own. *He does not want us to accomplish through coercion and impersonal laws what we should be accomplishing through laying down our lives for others.* Until we learn this, we are going to keep on circling Mount Sinai.

If we are ever to win our world for Jesus Christ in any arena, we must go beyond the uneasy tension between activism and politics to true Christianity: a faith that is a pearl of great price worth trading all to obtain. Operation Rescue poked into our tents the camel's nose of what it means to live like a Christian in only one small part of the American culture. The rest of that hairy, smelly camel is terrifying to us if we consider the pattern of the Cross for dealing with pornography, drugs, government schools, ever-expanding government "solutions" to social problems, national and personal debt, and the government's battle to control Church schools, Church hiring practices, and even the list of sins we can preach against. In all these arenas we have been too willing to cooperate with whatever the world wants to do *if they would only leave us alone for the moment to raise nice Christian families in nice churches, and permit us to murmur politely against their abominations.*

In Rescue there is a clear pattern of the Cross which applies to every area of Christian life. The only problem is, this pattern

runs counter to everything America has taught the Church about
how the successful Christian life ought to be lived. The Cross
not only runs counter to all forms of cooperation with evil, but
it runs counter to how we want to deal with evil should we
decide to try.

American Christians are too often caught between two
inadequate alternatives: being "spiritual" on the one hand, and
being an "activist" on the other. I wish I could find Biblical
support for either of these extremes. But there are no such
comfortable solutions in the Scriptures. The support for these
extremes comes from the American way, which calls us either to
the soul-warping personal peace and prosperity of do-nothing
spirituality, or to the all-consuming, life-warping, ideological
excitement of the battle which is activism. God preserve the
Church from either one, or from an illegitimate union of the
two. And, like Christianity, the theological framework of
Rescue is neither of these.[2] Rescue is nothing less than the
warp and woof of Christianity. Christianity is the warp and
woof of true civilization — true government, true churches, true
families, true men and women — in covenant with the true and
living God for all their needs. Transforming the world, by
laying down your life, is the heart of Rescue. It is the heart of
evangelism. It is the heart of the Cross.

When you finish this book, my goal is not that you get arrested, but that you never again fear what men do to you. I want
you to set your affairs in order so that when it comes to obeying
God you do not make lawsuits, tax exemptions, going to jail,
losing your job, popularity, or success, your major
considerations.

This will take time. What are the first steps? Begin with

---

[2] The Church is to be characterized by both spirituality and an active
fervor to obey God in every arena. This includes intense times of spiritual
and devotional outpouring to God, as well as picketing, or canvassing a
neighborhood for a political race. But when the Church becomes
characterized by a mysticism which denies our responsibility before God
for His physical creation, she becomes irrelevant to His purposes in
history. And when the Church becomes lost in various crusades, though
seemingly relevant historically, she forgets her unique purpose and loses
her ability to bring heart-transforming Good News.

those areas where you can die to yourself in order to transform the part of the world God has entrusted to *you*. Most of us were not ready to die to ourselves to protect children from abortion/murder, because we have not died to ourselves in the mundane areas of dish washing, careers, report writing, finances, obeying our parents, making up our beds, picking up our own socks, tithing, being Christian businessmen. We were husbands who did not reflect Christ — that is, dying for our wives that they might stand resplendent in all their gifts, free to build the future. Or we were wives who rejected God's offer to fruitfully establish the future and instead chose to be someone else's secretary and "fulfill" ourselves. Begin here, but do not stop here. Continue to risk as you reach out to others.

If you are serious about winning your society to Jesus Christ, then Operation Rescue has many lessons to teach you. After 1989, Operation Rescue as a movement stalled. But, had we succeeded in the first push to overwhelm child-killing, what would we have done with our success? Can we afford "success" built on short-term commitment and fever-pitch, crisis, crisis, crisis excitement? Would it be success to seize the mere external reins of power and change a law temporarily whether through political or social activism? I think not. But the long-term seeds which Operation Rescue planted are growing.

Those seeds will result in a movement of people who will be instruments of true heart change — a change evidenced in our willingness to lose everything for what is right and true — a willingness to serve. Seeking change through activism, the normal political process, revolution, or prayer and preaching, cannot replace laying down your life in obedience to God.

I believe the days of ten-thousand-person Rescues are still ahead. I believe we will see huge crowds of Christians descend on free-standing clinics and each take a brick home with them. I know for a fact that most abortionists expect this of us. But it will require a tremendous spiritual transformation in each of us for this to be not only a possible but a positive step. This transformation in the Church will come as a result of enough Christians trading their lives for others, thereby purchasing the right to speak to our society. The power to serve is the power to rule. When we learn to serve, then our whole society, not just its abortion laws, will lie open to be transformed by the Gospel.

If our goal is not to transform society, but just tinker with it, then we will fail. God is playing for keeps. If we want to take back the power bases of our society, we must first learn to lay down our lives in service. If we want to continue in Biblical authority in society, we will only do so by sacrificial example. A power base not built on laying down our lives, is fit only for destruction, not recovery. As Jesus said in Matthew 20:25, "The rulers of the Gentiles lord it over them. And those who are great exercise authority over them. Yet it shall not be so among you; but whoever desires to be great among you, let him be your servant, and whoever desires to be first among you let him be your slave — just as the Son of Man did not come to be served, but to serve, and to give His life as a ransom for many."

The Church in America must again become the Church of Jesus Christ. Not a social crusade. Not an inquisition. Not a mass evangelism rally. Not a recruiting pool for activist and political issues. Not a spiritual bath-house where Christians huddle to keep out the world, only to contract spiritual AIDS and die emaciated shadows of what God intended. Not even a think-tank. Rather, we must become functioning Christians in functioning churches, unafraid to lose everything as we live like Christ when we reach out to a lost world.

Someone will have to begin. While it may be a first step for many of us, it is only our first step down an old, well-worn path, trod by the Church through the ages. Is God calling you to take your first steps with that company of saints? If so, stopping child-killing may not even be the arena you lose your life in. But wherever it is, God calls you to continue down that path. This is the crisis of the Cross in America: can we die in order to live, fail in order to succeed? Can we love God with all our heart and love our neighbor as our selves in deed as well as word? Not *can* we, but *will* we, shatter the darkness?

Joseph L. Foreman
Fulton County Jail
Atlanta, Georgia
1991

SECTION I

THE PRINCIPLES

AND

PRACTICE OF THE CROSS

In all arenas of life, we have strayed so far from our heritage of sacrificial obedience to God, that peacefully stopping a baby-murderer seems extreme. Because we do not Rescue in any area of life, Rescue at an abortion clinic seems pushy. Face it: Rescuers — that is to say, Christians — *are* pushy where life and death or heaven and hell are at stake. The Cross does not wait until a more polite, humane era when people can be crucified with their clothes on, and take anesthesia for the pain. We take up our cross, period. If you do not take it up where God has called you, that "humane era" will never come.

So consider the rock from which you were hewn.

Chapter 1

WHAT IS RESCUE?

The Challenge to God's Name

In 1960, there was a day when the Sons of God came to present themselves before the LORD, and Satan also came among them. And the LORD said to him, "From where do you come?"

So Satan answered Him, "From going to and fro on the earth and from walking back and forth on it."

Then the LORD said to Satan, "Have you considered My servant the American Church, how there is none like them in all the earth for seminaries, missionaries, budgets, buildings and programs to advance My kingdom, how they fear God and shun evil?"

So Satan said, "Do they fear God for nothing? Look at them. You have given them everything they could possibly want, you have hedged them about. They do not love *you*, they love the things you have given them. They worship your blessings."

"Yes?"

"I will not say that I can get them to curse you to your face — I failed with Job. But, I will say this: your people are incapable of even the most basic acts of Christian faith and charity — acts by which you yourself said that others could determine the difference between your children and My children, your sheep and My goats."

"Yes?"

"Yes," said Satan. "You say your people follow you like sheep? Within thirty years, you will not be able to get so much as one Christian to follow you across the street to save a baby's life. Then you will have to turn, remove their lampstand, and visit their land with a curse."

In 1973, *Roe v. Wade* struck down all anti-abortion laws in America, creating the "right" of all women to hire a doctor to kill their children at any time during the full nine months before birth. Its companion decision, *Doe v. Bolton*, on the same day

3

decreed that a woman could do so for any reason.

And no Christian could be found to so much as cross the street to physically intervene for these children. And the slaughter grew quickly to 4,500 a day. It became a slaughter carried out in most hospitals and in publicly advertised clinics, established to make the killing quick and easy for everyone. So acceptable did it become, that Christians would go to child-murdering hospitals, or buy everyday necessities — from phone calls and Cheerios to toilet paper — from companies who helped promote child-killing organizations. Most Christian women thought nothing of having their children delivered by the same doctor who would be as willing to kill their children. Pastors feared rebuke from their congregations if they mentioned the "A" word too often — or at all.

Again, in 1989, there was a day when the Sons of God came to present themselves before the LORD, and Satan also came among them. And the LORD said to Him, "From where do you come?"

So Satan answered Him, "From going to and fro on the earth and from walking back and forth on it."

Then the LORD said to Satan, "Have you considered My servant the American Church? Fifty thousand have crossed the street and physically protected a generation yet unborn, though you incite Me against them to destroy them without cause."

"Skin for skin!" answered Satan. "Touch their houses, their church buildings, their families, their careers, their savings. Threaten them physically with beatings by police, long jail sentences, beatings and AIDS-infested urine from pro-abortion demonstrators. Then you will see them abandon your command to love and serve you only, as they scramble to abandon their neighbor to save themselves. They are My children, not yours. You will see the very Christians who spoke the loudest in defense of rescuing the babies become the leaders in justifying, in your own name, why they should no longer physically protect them, but seek some other way to 'rescue' them. You will see them bow and worship the same gods the feminists, the mothers seeking abortion, and the doctors worship — the gods of Respectability, Autonomy, Career, Self-preservation. They will cry out to these new gods to preserve their organizations, reputations, and bank accounts — even those of the Rescue organizations themselves. In that day your people will knowingly allow My doctors to offer Me sacrifices of the fruit of the womb. Your people will allow these sacrifices to buy the peace, prosperity, and blessings they crave — blessings they will never trust you to bestow.[3] To preserve their way of life at all cost, they will make peace with Me."

* * * *

Job never did get a clear revelation of the divine issues at stake in his life. He just lived with integrity and let God be God. All saints in their hour of testing experience this same mystery. Their purpose and vision only seem clear as *we* look back on the battles *they* fought. Like them, we can never get a clear look at what is at stake in our battles. But we must obey God anyway, and hope that as future generations stand on our shoulders, God's purpose in us will be clear to them. When thousands of children are killed daily in our presence, what could it be other than a divine question being asked of each of us?

Can it be that so much more is at stake than a sinner's right to be legally sinful? More than just the lives of the children? Perhaps even the integrity of the NAME of God in His people? To find out, we need to understand correctly what Rescue is, and compare it to what Christianity is. The intent of Operation Rescue was to lay the reality of abortion bare before the nation in distinctly Christian terms: *"If abortion is murder, then let's act like it and let God be God!"*

Three Problems

Before Operation Rescue launched the idea of Rescue around the nation, we spent a year and a half hammering out precisely what we did and did not want to do, and exactly how to explain it. Yet even with the greatest care, there were problems woven into the fabric of our effort. I believe that the purpose of Rescue is not only right, but crucial to the very

---

[3] Hosea 2:5, 8-9.

continuation of any civilization. But to move forward, three practical problems we encountered must be addressed.

1) *Rescue is not so much in need of defense as it is in need of definition.* Too often I have been told that Rescue is wrong, only to hear any number of other activities described which are not "Rescue." Operation Rescue was launched without a clear definition of Rescue itself. This is not to say books were not written arguing for it; they were. But the questions remained: "What is it about *sitting-in* which is special? Is there something uniquely compelling for Christians about *these* particular tactics? Why should the Church do *this*, when there are many ways to 'rescue' the preborn?"

2) *We built two defining focal points into Operation Rescue: "Save a baby at any cost," and "Create political clout to change the law."* Neither of these taken alone is wrong. But together, they became separate masters defining the purpose of a Rescue. They created an unresolvable internal conflict. Put most simply, if our purpose is to *save a life*, then even one person walking into the death camp is reasonable as long as it is the best you could put forth that day — Missionaries to the Preborn follow this by trying to rescue every day they are out of jail, even if alone. But, if our purpose is to *create a movement*, then our actions will be legitimated to the extent that they generate media, numbers, and popularity — though saving a life *is* important, it would be the publicity of our event which made Rescue right. The lack of focus created by the confusion of these two purposes — the prophetic and the kingly — has led to much woe. But neither is wrong. They simply cannot definitively shape the same event. One will dominate and the other be violated. This has been the key tension within the Rescue movement, and more broadly in the Church itself.

3) *The way we set forth the case of the children — the way we declared our willingness to defend them — left us with a win-or-die stand.* The problem was not that we had some unique or strident position which could be corrected by better wording. We had simply restated the historic position of the Church: "Abortion is murder of the innocent, and it is the responsibility of every decent Christian to defend the innocent." If this is true, then we could neither go back on our description of the situation

when popularity waned, nor could many afford to lose their freedom, jobs, family, and houses by continuing to rescue at all cost. We — particularly the leaders — were publicly caught between what we promised and what we could deliver.

These three problems were built into Operation Rescue from the foundation. They are the rocks we grounded on when those hostile to the sacrifice of Rescue looked for any unevenness or straw man to attack.

What You Can Expect to See at a Rescue

But before we go into these things, do you know what the act itself is which Operation Rescue made famous, calling it "Rescue?" We must start here because this simple act led every part of the pro-life movement to use the concept of "Rescue" to justify and describe its own actions. Sidewalk counselors and picketers "Rescue" children by persuading mothers to go away. Crisis Pregnancy Centers "Rescue" the children of the mothers they counsel. Educators "Rescue" the children of future pregnancies by encouraging chastity and informing people about the nature of human development in the womb and the horror of abortion. Even political activists are "Rescuing" those children who will be protected by the laws which in coming years will prohibit some or all forms of child-killing in the womb. Most pro-life fund raising is now marked with this promise: "Your dollars will go toward saving babies from abortion." Perhaps more than any other testimony, this affirms the fundamental rightness of the simple act which got *everyone* to think of themselves as Rescuers in the first place. So what was that act?

A Rescue is when one or more people use their passive yet physical presence to prevent others from killing children at an abortion clinic. Usually this involves kneeling in front of the door so that no one can get in. In some Rescues people enter the building, pray in the killing chambers, or talk with the mothers who are waiting to have their children killed. To slow down their removal, Rescuers will sometimes lock themselves together or to something in the death camp with case-hardened steel bicycle locks. Sometimes they will render the murder weapon harmless by damaging or destroying the suction aspiration machine and desterilizing instruments.

While the doors are blocked, other Christians stand outside to meet the mothers coming for their appointments with death. As long as the mothers cannot get in, they have the opportunity to hear about the reality of abortion and are offered compassionate, caring alternatives. In almost every Rescue one or two mothers will change their minds directly and not kill their children. Many more will drive by and never return. Even more see the news on TV and decide, before ever getting pregnant, that abortion is not worth it.[4]

The common thread in all Rescues is that child-killing is made impossible by Christians who are physically, but harmlessly, preventing it — standing in solidarity with the unborn.

The Rescue often ends with the arrest of the Christians. But arrest is never the purpose of a Rescue, nor is a Rescue's primary purpose to challenge the legal or political system. That is why we always speak of *"risking* arrest," instead of "going out to get arrested." Christians who rescue will rise to whatever legal or political challenge comes their way following the Rescue, but their heart is in saving lives by physically, but non-violently, preventing the killing. The power of their challenge to the legal-political system and the clarity of their witness to the saving power of Jesus Christ depends on the focused purity of the Rescue itself — it rests on trying to save a particular baby scheduled for execution *today* and letting the chips fall where they may.

It is important to grasp the simplicity of Rescue. Often when people argue about Rescue, those against it are arguing against sit-ins which break the law. Those arguing for it are urging us to prophetically imitate Christ whose name — Yeshua — means "Savior," "Rescuer." It is not hard to see why a sit-

---

[4] Our experience in the siege of the Atlanta death camps in 1988 proved that weekly Rescues cut into the killing business, dramatically eliminating almost 70% of it even on days when no Rescue was scheduled. In the year following that time, abortion clinic personnel report that their abortion business was only 50% of what it was before July 18, 1988. What was even more impressive was the fact that the client load of all Crisis Pregnancy Centers in a hundred mile radius increased dramatically, as did the 75% voter turnout in Georgia in the 1988 general elections. This spells saved lives and changing hearts. Other sieges have had similar results.

in does not seem to carry the same prophetic weight as the name
of our Lord. This book is about Rescue in the grand scheme of
God's plan, as well as about blocking doors. Therefore, when
we refer to "Rescue," we mean the broader principles of the
Cross reflected in a simple act of obedience to God, such as
blocking the doors of an abortion clinic, or loving your wife, or
feeding the hungry, or preaching the Gospel. The arrest, the
prayer, the suffering, the prison, the fear, the challenge to the
legal powers of darkness in this age; these things will grow out
of any Rescue which has been made illegal. Where abortion is
concerned, the Rescue itself is when a mother comes and fails to
kill her child because Christians would not let her in that day,
and her heart was moved to spare her own child.

The growing awareness that the pro-life movement is a
Rescue Movement is entirely correct, for many other things do
indeed "Rescue" children — picketing, prayer, sermons, burning
down the high place, changing laws, and properly loving and
raising our children. These other actions demand sacrifice to be
effective. The very fact that everyone is so quick to pick up the
name indicates the very truth we wished it to convey, and the
legitimacy of any action which truly represents it. The fact that
we would protect children through persuasion, legal action, and
protest only amplifies the fact that it is right to protect them
physically by keeping children away from killers. Because we
recognize the validity of Rescue itself in the grand sense, we can
recognize all these activities as being Rescues in a derivative
sense. Ironically, our blocking of doors opened this whole
perspective to us. And that is what this book is all about: the
connection between Rescue at the abortion clinic kneel-in, and
Rescue in every sense — the Christian life, or being a citizen of
God's kingdom.

So We Tried Door Blocking as a New Strategy . . .

When we began to rescue, we got arrested. "Now what?"
we wondered. "Do we do it again? Did we try to save lives
just to make our point? Or is physically protecting children a
normal way of life for Christians?" We decided it was worth
trying again and again. But still, at that time, Rescue in our
minds was a strategy. It was not proposed as a normal way of

life for a Christian.

The courts understand civil disobedience as a strategy. To make sure that we keep it a mere strategy, the courts and police will beat us, throw us in jail, or seize our property in lawsuits. The courts want to intimidate us out of protecting children again. They are happy to let us make our point, but want us to stop after one or two times. The world's idea is that protecting children before they are born is, even for Christians, a mere political issue. They do not believe that we will act as if children in the womb are equal to us just because God tells us they are. The world does not believe that Christians will go to jail for a few years in order to give a child the chance to live out his whole three score and ten. The suffering with which society threatens us becomes their intimidating yardstick for our faith: "How much suffering is that little life worth? How much suffering is God's Name worth? How much suffering is God's Word worth?"

For the most part, the strategy of the abortion culture and its courts has been successful. They discovered that we were only prepared to treat preborn children as equals in theory, but not as equals in real life. Therefore, we drew back. We were not prepared at this time to "love not our lives unto death" — or even much jail. For that matter, we were not even prepared to "endure joyfully the seizure of our property."[5] Are the children's lives really worth risking the loss of everything?

The abortion culture has laid its cards on the table and called our hand: "If you really believe they are human, why do you spend so much of your life acting as if you don't?" They ask us, "Why don't you picket every day, much less rescue every day? Why don't you bomb these 'death chambers' as you call them? Why not open *your* home to unwed mothers?" These are not unreasonable questions. They stem from Christian rhetoric. We must ask, "Is defending innocent human life a special calling or a universal obligation? Is it a strategy or a way of life? Is it what we do when it is convenient or is it fundamental to Christianity and civilization?" We have called it

---

[5] Revelation 12:11; Hebrews 10:32-39.

fundamental, yet treated it as a neat strategy. Which is it?

Even though today most Christians will not lay down their lives and suffer for others in any ministry, I believe that this will change in the next few years. Until then, a few Christians will risk losing everything to rescue even one child, or one marriage, or one reputation, or one church from splitting, or one soul from hell. That is the cost of clearing a road for the world to follow. While this road is very old and well-established, in our day it has become badly eroded and overgrown. It can be resurveyed with our words; but it can only be cleared and repaved with our lives, as it was by the lives of the saints and martyrs who went before us. For those who are rediscovering this road today, the Rescue does not end with the arrest and a kangaroo court's conviction. The Rescue continues as Christians become witnesses[6] throughout the legal system. They declare with their lives what the saints have always declared: "There is only one God and we will love and serve Him at any cost" — in this case, we will not cooperate with the protection of murder.

More and more Christians who continue to Rescue do not do so because of the strategic possibility of saving a few lives in a way that enables them to keep their jobs, houses, and churches, while making a large media impact, and stirring up political pressure. They rescue because it is right. They ask: "If it is right to physically save a life, then will I let a legal system make me act like it is wrong?" In other words, "Will I go back to acting as if the unborn are no longer worthy of my protection?" Whenever the legal system is through with its punishment, whether jail, fines, or probation, will they find us again physically standing between the abortionist and his tiny victims? Will Christians ever learn? Learn what? Learn that it is right to join the state in its protection of murder?

No. They will never learn this.

. . . And Found in Rescue the Christian Way of Life

To answer the world, many have had to reject Christian compassion as a strategy, and to replace it with Christian

---

[6] The Greek for this word is often brought directly into English as *Martyr*.

compassion as a way of life. A pastor in Milwaukee summed up this commitment as he stood before a local judge for the 45th time. The judge asked, "Reverend Trewhella, aren't you ever going to get tired of this? When will you quit?" To which the pastor replied, "When are you going to quit being a judge? You chose your career because it was a good one and you probably plan to keep it as long as you can. That's how I feel about protecting children from butchers. It's a worthy way to spend the rest of my life, and I plan to do so until they are safe. I'm a minister of the gospel, what else would you expect of me?" Here is a new kind — or should I say, a refreshingly old kind — of Christian emerging.

Rescue is the cutting edge of the Church's compassionate intolerance toward legalized child-killing, even as taking up a cross is the Christian's compassionate intolerance of evil in every arena. It is not a crusade. It is about laying down your life again and again and again and again until this or any holocaust is over. It is only out of a population marked by repentance, intolerance to murder, open hearts, and homes to provide loving alternatives, that laws will spring forth with sufficient power and clarity to rid us of both legalized child murder and the supporting culture which so readily accepts killing the weak or "unfit" as the solution to society's problems. This example of sacrificial obedience to God scarcely exists in the American Church. We will never transform our culture by politicking for a surface change in the law. Change will only come from the example of Christians who are not afraid to live what they believe — who would rather lose every church, house, and job they have than to go down in history as the Christians who presided over the greatest human carnage in the history of the world. Such Christians will never prefer to rescue their things instead of their neighbors.

When we dabbled with Rescue, we found that, as a strategy, it was fun at first, but costly in the end. As a way of life . . . well, it is becoming very dangerous to every*thing* we hold dear in this life. Will enough Christians embrace simple, compassionate Christianity for the Gospel to get a hearing in our churches and in our land? If enough do, then revival and dramatic change will be possible.

The Crisis of the Cross

Of course we know that protecting a baby is one of those fundamental requirements of life. Protecting the lives of babies may be among the fundamental issues of any society and even a watershed test of faith in the living God.[7] Protecting innocent children is not "activism." It is one of the deeper implications of orthodox Christianity as it is displayed not only in Rescue, but in the very possibility of civilization, law, order, prosperity, civil rights, and every other good and perfect gift God offers any human society. The question is, how can sit-ins partake in this heritage? This is where a definition of Rescue itself is sorely needed, in both the narrow as well as in the universal sense.

In the early days of Operation Rescue we tended to limit our argument for Rescue to the fulfillment of the second great summary of the Law, "Love your neighbor as yourself." We did not state clearly enough that loving God is the first and greatest issue facing the Church in our country. Will we love God though it costs us everything?

This may seem judgmental, but I believe that there is an acid test: If an all-consuming love for God characterized our churches, then the cost of lawsuits and prisons would never have intimidated us. We would have not sought out nor clung to strategies which were "safer" or "wiser" than Rescue. Had we considered the value of that blood which bought us in all other areas of our lives and ministries, we would laugh at the paltry counter-offers the world made for our souls. We would never join with them to protect abortion/murder, instead of protecting the babies being murdered. "Give us your soul and we won't sue you, give us your soul and we won't send you to jail. Give us your soul and you can preach the Gospel freely," the world murmurs soothingly. We would have joined God in laughing in derision at His enemies. Did they think so little of our Lord and His Cross that they thought they could get us to defend child-

---

[7] Matthew 25:31-46 "Inasmuch as you did not do it to one of the least of these, you did not do it to *Me*." The issue here is separating sheep from goats, God's children from Satan's. What is more fundamental than God's ability to recognize who belongs to His flock and who are of the devil's flock disguised as His? (See also footnote 8, on page 75.)

killing with them and sell out our Lord for fear of a few beatings, jail time, and loss of property from lawsuits?

Yet, instead of dealing with the grand issue of Rescue — love the Lord with all your heart, soul, mind, and strength — the Church chose to bog down in petty arguments about strategies and tactics. We wondered if this or that form of activism was better than this or that form of prayer and politicking.

The reason so many Christian leaders cannot see the relationship between blocking the doors of a death camp and the broader Rescue ministry of the Church, is that in American society we have all but abandoned the broader costly ministry of Jesus Christ.[8] We follow a "jesus" who cannot say "No!" to the comforts of this life — church building projects, homes in the suburbs, and a well-paying job to support these "necessary" blessings of the kingdom of God.

Do we make such accusations because the Church does not do sit-ins at abortion clinics? No! It is because there are supposed to be 50 million born-again Christians in America — yet even so, the inner city is still a growing cancer. Our government has become bloated and godless. Almost every power base in our nation — media, arts, education, government, even prominent segments of the Church itself — is self-consciously non- or anti-Christian. We have almost lost a generation to hedonism and drugs. Our testimony to a God Who rules all is so feeble that even in our beloved suburbs our own neighbors have not seen in our lives sufficient witness to the power of a God who saves so as to have their lives changed in any significant numbers. These things testify against us. The fact that we do not sit-in at an abortion clinic is only one of a flood of shortcomings. As Jesus told His church in Revelation 3:17, "You say, 'I am rich and have become wealthy, and have

---

[8] Hostility to Rescue is located predominately in the leadership of the Church, not in the rank and file Christian. My wife and I discovered this as we were trying to find a home to rent in Atlanta so we could continue rescuing there with Missionaries to the Preborn. We were direct with every potential landlord about our calling as missionaries to the preborn and income situation. We discovered, in a city which was perhaps the coldest toward Rescue as far as pastors are concerned, a warm support and respect without exception from all we sought to rent from.

need of nothing' — and do not know that you are wretched, miserable, poor, blind and naked."

In Hebrews 11:35 ff., the writer describes how God's people chose to be "tortured, not accepting release, because they looked for a better resurrection . . . they were sawn in half, scourged, imprisoned . . . they wandered in sheepskins and goatskins, living in holes in the ground." This level of commitment simply has not characterized our faith at any level. So how could any of us have been expected to sacrifice to protect and provide for children in the womb and their mothers? If we are unable to be called "people of whom the world was not worthy . . . whom God was not ashamed to be called their God,"[9] then, how could we be expected to see the relationship between our faith and the lives of the children?

I do not say these things to look back and berate us for our prior blindness. Rather, let's look ahead and ask, "How long will we use the excuses we had when we *first* realized how much we would have to sacrifice, to justify why we cannot leave all and follow the Lord *now*?" Where is the offense of the Cross in American Christianity? What will stop you from losing everything for our Lord today, or a year from now? When will your neighbor see you following a God worth living for, the God Whose orders are worth suffering and dying for?

When we get to the heart of it, Rescue is putting God first by obeying Him when He tells us to put others first. Rescue is doing it in a way which sacrifices our benefit and comfort for another's, whether on the mission field, in our churches, in our marriages, in our careers, or at the abortion factories. Rescue is when we physically intervene to protect someone in a way which does not hurt anyone and which causes us to throw in our lot, our reputation, and our future with the one whose life has been declared refuse: we become refuse with him in the name of Christ who became refuse for us. A sit-in may do this, as may starting a home for unwed mothers, being scrupulously honest in your business practices, defending someone whose reputation is being savaged behind his back, or just saying, "I'm

---

[9] Hebrews 11:16,38.

sorry," to your wife, husband, or child. In all these ways we stand for others, therefore we may call them "Rescues." In rescuing others we find that we are rescued ourselves from the idols we use to justify and preserve our good life — the ones which prevent us from responding to the sacrifice of truth, justice, mercy, or infants, going on where we live, work, and worship.

Many people will encourage you to take up the Cross in your singing, preaching, praying, venerating those who took it up long ago, and in your daydreams. But the same people who encourage you to take up the Cross in these ways will be the first to discourage you from taking it up in real life. All you treasure will cry out to you along with your well-meaning friends to leave the Cross alone, to let it remain a powerful symbol, but not to let it rob you of all you have. For when you take up the Cross, all things become captive to Jesus Christ — the idols which rule the nation and those which rule much of our lives — and are led captive in procession behind the Cross.[10]

---

[10] In Colossians 2:13-15 Paul pictures the wild victory procession of Christ in terms of the conquering Roman generals leading their booty and slaves through the Roman streets. Christ did this on the Cross and calls us to join in this victory procession by taking up the Cross which is to mark both our justification — His nailing of our sins and their power over us to the Cross — and our sanctification — His empowering us to lead lives of holiness and purity, laid down for others, in His Name. The Cross is the destruction of self-service. It is the epitome of service to others. This is why all solutions to abortion — including rescuing — must clear away the idols of self-service or in the end they will become merely nice variations of idolatry. What makes something — even a good thing in and of itself — an idol? Seeking to preserve it at any cost to our soul, to the lives of the children, and to His Name. See also, Ephesians 4:8; Colossians 2:15; I Corinthians 4:6-14, esp v 9.

Chapter 2

THE THEOLOGICAL ROOT OF RESCUE

Ethics Must Be More Than Spontaneity

On the coldest day of 1984 a small child wandered out the front door of our house, dragging her snow suit behind her. She walked half a block up the windswept Philadelphia street and looked both ways before walking into the middle of the busy intersection.

It was below zero, and the wind chill made it thirty to forty degrees deadlier than that. There she was — standing pitifully in the middle of the intersection, holding her little coat, too cold even to cry. Only her nose ran. Did the traffic stop? No, their careers and lives called them on that morning and they rode past on either side as she stood there. No one felt led of God to help this child. God understood why there was really nothing any of them could do. He had given each passerby an important ministry and call that morning.

I remember it so vividly because she was supposed to be my responsibility. My wife had been baby-sitting and she had stepped out for a moment and left the front door unlocked by mistake. The little girl had tried to follow her a few minutes later. By the time she was in the street I was searching the house frantically.

I'm sure if you had driven by that day you would have immediately stopped your car. You would have risked breaking the law by walking out into traffic, and even blocking the whole intersection until the girl was safe — she was not even two years old. You would have had some angry thoughts about whoever was so careless of innocent, trusting little ones. You would not have checked yourself to repent of those hostile thoughts aimed at me. You would not have felt like a hero, but you would have been shocked to think that anyone could argue against you or condemn you. You would laugh at the idea that blocking the whole intersection could be compared to the civil rights activists who did the same thing in the sixties. You would be stunned to hear that leading Christian pastors looked down on you because you brought a child to safety, instead of doing the Christian thing — prophetically standing by the edge of the street and preaching powerfully to the cars as they drove past, or perhaps breaking a pot as Jeremiah did, to symbolize what God would do to such a careless generation. You would be amazed if leading Christian thinkers scoffed at you because you did not stop to consult with them to gain a proper perspective and analysis of when someone should or should not break the law. You would not write a treatise called, *The Theology of Rescuing Small Children in the Street*. You would not have started a movement called "Operation Rescue." You would have just Rescued. Unfortunately, you were not driving by that morning.

Operation Rescue was like that for many of us. We stopped driving by and rushed across the street to the brink of death and saved their lives. Unlike the little girl I was responsible for, however, it is no oversight that brings the helpless babies to the clinic. Our abortion culture is dead serious about killing; when we get nervous about their threats, it is hard to remember why we wanted to Rescue in the first place. If we cannot respond in simple, spontaneous Christian compassion, can we still respond? Were our instincts to Rescue correct, or just emotionalism? These are the questions which the continuing attempt to protect the people in the womb raises for all Christians. Whether Rescuing a child in the street, or in the womb, we see a striking example of true Christianity in daily practice.

Rescue: The Heartbeat of Faith

Why did fifty-five thousand Christians get arrested with Operation Rescue over the last few years? Some argue that they took to heart what actually happens to the child if no one tries to rescue him. Others say that sixteen years of frustration were waiting to ignite. But there is more to Rescue than publicity and the serious demonstration of commitment; more than the opportunity to challenge bad laws in the branch of government which spawned them — the judiciary; more than the attempt to save a mother from being exploited and her child from being killed. Beyond these lay much deeper the true heart and root of Rescue, emanating from the center of our Christian faith. We did it for the same reason you would have rescued that little girl in the traffic — you are a creature in God's image, and so is she.[1]

Rescue showed people that saving a baby's life is as normal and expected a part of a Christian life as church attendance, prayer, and Bible reading. People understood that to refuse to save a child whom we could have saved is to incur the guilt of innocent blood. People saw that even though saving a life may lead them to break the traditions of men — falsely called "law" in this society[2] — saving an innocent life is *not* breaking a law, no matter what the policemen and judges of this age might think. God, not man, still defines law.[3] Those who Rescued understood these things, but it still does not get to the heart of Rescue.

There is no end of arguments which try to balance Romans 13 with Biblical examples of godly obedience in the teeth of evil government decrees — Daniel, Moses, the Prophets, and Apostles. Yet few who accepted — or rejected — Rescue did so based on these arguments. At the bottom of it all is one simple fact explaining both why people Rescue as well as flee Rescue: *Rescue resonates with the deepest heart-beat of what it means to be a child of God, by challenging us to take up a cross.* This explains its attraction — what Christian does not want to respond joyfully to that which touches the wellsprings of his life?

But taking up a cross is as repellent as it is attractive. By challenging us to the core it exacts a price. It uncovers a willingness to coexist peacefully with the vilest evil. Even as we rescue, we discover our overwhelming desire to keep the comfortable tokens of our faith around us — a nice home, a job, and freedom to worship. Until Rescue we could honestly say, "What can I do about *this* child being killed today?"[4] We also feared the consequences to ourselves of the only other real solution to child-killers we could think of — "Do unto them before they get a chance to do unto the little ones."

---

[1] There were ignoble reasons as well: a few wanted to punish the system, and others had an internal need for excitement. A little jail cured both.

[2] Luke 6:6-11.

[3] Romans 13:1-7. Paul limits the legitimate authority of government to doing good. And who defines the "good" government is limited to?

[4] Proverbs 24:12, "If you say, 'But we knew nothing about this,' . . ."

What Did Jesus Do?

People rescue because it agrees with almost everything the Church and the Scriptures have proven to be true in theory as well as in practice. Protecting an innocent child from dismemberment, in a way which offers compassionate help to his mother, strikes a deep chord in the life of Christ and His Church because it is not what Jesus *would* do; it is what Jesus *did* do. He Rescued. Did He become a political activist? Did He lobby? Did He help only those who could find His name in the yellow pages? Did Jesus picket? Did He only preach and pray? Did He even visit John the Baptist in jail? Did He start hospitals? Did He run for king, or Caesar? No, His Name is *Rescue*. That is what He did, and that is what He continues to do.

Jesus went to the heart of the matter — He personally took up His Cross to shield us. On that Cross, in our place, He suffered and died. Foolish? Yes. From the perspective of Peter's plans for Him — the perspective of big crowds, big crowns, big budgets, big building programs with cushioned pews — very foolish.[5] Yet it is where Jesus put the center of His ministry, and He says, "The servant is not greater than his master." In the end, His pattern is the only pattern for any ministry that calls itself Christian: "Whoever does not bear his cross and come after Me, cannot be My *disciple*." In this light, hear His last command: "Go make *disciples* of all nations."[6] For these unborn neighbors, their only knowledge of the Cross in this life will be when those who claim to bear it dare to defend them from the butcher who seeks their life and your soul.

The Three Principles of the Cross

Three facts about the Cross define Rescue:

1) **The Atonement of Christ:** *It is an act of physical intervention.* The greatest preacher of all time did not save us by His words alone. The greatest man of prayer did not emerge from Gethsemane at two in the morning and say, "It is finished." When Peter tried to take the Cross out of our Lord's

---

[5] Matthew 16:21-27; I Corinthians 1:18 ff.

[6] John 15:20; Luke 14:26-27; Matthew 28:19.

ministry, Jesus called him Satan. Jesus did not just talk about physically intervening on behalf of the helpless, He did it. *He Rescued us.* Had He simply proven His dedication at the Cross by going up to it, but walking away at the last minute (thus delivering Himself from death) we would not be saved. It was not Jesus' arrest and walk to Golgatha which saved us, it was the physical intervention of the Cross itself — from that point, Jesus stopped walking. That is why we stop walking when we get to the point of physical intervention — not our arrest, but our blocking the door. His substitutionary atonement not only saves us, it is the pattern of the way of life for which we have been saved — our take-up-your-cross-and-follow-Me example for life — directing us to physically stand in the path of deadly harm intended for others.

2) **The Submission of Christ:** *He was harmless toward His enemies and took destruction to Himself.* Had He not submitted to the Father, He could never have stood in our place. Had He fought back He could not have stood in our place, so He harmed neither soldier nor priest. He had to submit; He had to be *harmless* to take the wrath in our place — who could force Him to do it? If we did not submit to protecting others voluntarily as He did, who could force us? They will not arrest us in our homes and churches, because there we do not stand for anyone other than ourselves. Jesus did not swerve from His submission and come down from the Cross. This is why we go limp instead of assisting in the murder by walking away (if we walked we would no longer be harmless toward the children). We resist without fighting back when we stand in the path of destruction for the child, his mother, and our society.

3) **The Incarnation of Christ:** *He identified with us.* God became flesh. Then He became sin. He did not rescue from afar. He personally took on our helpless estate. The Cross illuminates His incarnation: "Do not reject them, reject Me." He bore our rejection in His person.[7] He then calls us to bear the rejection of others and so minister to Him: "Inasmuch as you do it to the least of these, you do it unto Me . . . Have in

---

[7] Isaiah 53.

you the mind which was in Christ Jesus . . . Let us therefore go up with Him outside the camp, bearing His reproach."[8] Because we could not save ourselves, He refused to walk away and save Himself. This is the incarnation as *we* are to practice it. We throw in our lot with the fatherless, the widow, the stranger, and the poor, imitating Him Who threw in His lot with us.[9]

Rescue brings these three principles together into one action: 1) we physically intervene, 2) in a way that does not harm anyone, 3) taking on punishment and judgement to ourselves so that children and their mothers (not to mention the doctors and police) might live. Rescue is not any one or two of these three principles. It is the activity in which all three function equally to form the boundary of all Rescue tactics:

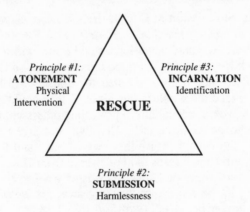

Principle #1:
ATONEMENT
Physical
Intervention

RESCUE

Principle #3:
INCARNATION
Identification

Principle #2:
SUBMISSION
Harmlessness

The Law of Love

If the incarnation and atonement are not enough to show what Rescue means in the Christian life, consider how Rescue embodies the two great summaries of the law. First, through the Cross Jesus Christ secured heirs who would love the Lord their God with *all* their heart, soul, mind, and strength. In other words, Christ saved us to be like Him and put no authority or standard higher than God's, regardless of the personal cost.

---

[8] Matthew 25:40; Philippians 2:3 ff; Hebrews 13:12-13.

[9] Philippians 2:3-8.

Second, in the Cross Jesus established the pattern of loving His neighbor as Himself by being His brother's keeper. He was no mere "righteous" bystander. He did not pass by on the other side. In the Cross God gave us the heart of all law which is binding on a Christian as a pattern for life — love of God and love of neighbor, regardless of cost. The Cross is God's final answer to evil.[10] Is it ours? Or is our answer to evil in this world limited to prayer meetings, bombs, picket signs, and politics? Surely we might be able to find a place for these, but what is our final answer? The Christian lays down his life for his preborn neighbor — the love of Christ compels him.

When it comes to preborn neighbors, this nation's judges and policemen interpret U.S. and state laws to say: "You shall *not* love your neighbor as yourself. Do *not* do unto others as you would have them do unto you. Love God in word only, but not with *all* your strength." But God says, "Be *not* conformed to this world, but be transformed . . . . Love the Lord your God with *all* your heart, soul, mind, and strength, and love your neighbor as yourself . . . . Do unto others as you would have them do unto you . . . . Inasmuch as you have done it unto the least of these you have done it unto Me . . . . For *all* who desire to live godly in Christ Jesus *will* suffer persecution."[11] Whose love will control our lives? Whose standards will guide our actions? Will we obey trespass laws and protect abortionists, or will we obey God and protect the preborn? Whom will we serve *today*?

Rescue then, is practical, basic Christianity. It reflects in one activity the atonement, the submission and incarnation of Christ, the law of love, and God's final authority. In the face of legalized human sacrifice the Rescuer rejects the lies of a secular world and raises the Cross. Here is his guide for behavior and hope for this generation: "Whoever wishes to make himself a friend of the world, makes himself an enemy of God."[12]

---

[10] John 19:30.

[11] Romans 12:1; Matthew 22:34-40; 7:12; 25:45; II Timothy 3:12.

[12] James 4:4; also I John 2:15. The Cross fulfills God's promise of Genesis 3:16, that He would never remove that hostility between the way

Rescuers hold fast what Christians have always understood about their faith — it is directly related to the fate of the real world they live in. If the Cross is the center point of history, as well as of the believer's faith and life, then until churches grasp and live by this principle of laying down their lives for others, they will be peripheral to God's work in history and remain infants in their faith. They will not see revival, only more innocent blood shed, more pornography, more messianic government, more mindless revolutions, more poverty, more cultural bankruptcy, and more conversions to dead faith. Without revival, our entire civilization hangs in the balance. Along with Chuck Colson, Francis Schaeffer, John Paul II and a host of others throughout time and from every sector of Christendom, let me say it again, emphatically, *without a revival which results in a change in the way Christians live and relate to society, the West is finished, fallen from within to a new barbarism.* So what is this call for revival? a call for more sit-ins? more activism? No, it is a call for compassionate, prophetic, godly obedience in every part of our community — to have the mind of Christ.

God willing, the Church will always call for us to break every compromise with evil in every arena where she is at war. That is Rescue. God willing, we will never use the fact that we cannot rescue in every arena as an excuse to run from laying down our lives in *any* arena. God willing, we will never hide our eyes, heart, and support from those who are persecuted for rescuing in any arena. The Church which will neither suffer itself, nor stand with its representatives who suffer, is a Church which cannot follow Christ.[13]

---

of life and the way of death, from between the woman's seed and the serpent's seed.

[13] Luke 9:57; Hebrews 10:32-36,39; 11; 12; 13:3; Matthew 5:10-12; 6:21; Acts 5:41-42; I Peter 3:13-18; 4:12-19; Revelation 2:8; 3:14-22; 21:8. It is difficult to find anything in the New Testament which says otherwise, though American Christianity has put forth a herculean effort to establish a monument on the cornerstone of Peter's confession in Matthew 16:22: "Far be it from you, Lord! This [crucifixion] shall not happen to you." But it is still written, *"Everyone* who wants to live a godly life in Christ Jesus will be persecuted." II Timothy 3:12.

Chapter 3

THE TACTICS AND GOALS OF RESCUE

Doctrines of Demons

Fulton County jail was going to be my home for the next several years, so I made the most of this phase of my missionary ministry to the unborn by ministering to the prisoners through extensive counseling and Bible study. Most of them, though mere shells of humanity, were precious. They had all prayed the sinner's prayer to accept Christ. They would go forward at every Sunday chapel service when a local pastor would come in to preach and give an invitation to invite Christ into their lives. And they would return to cell block 500 with the same foul vocabulary, foul humor, and dreams of sex and drugs. Throughout the week they would pray with me for God to do more than be invited to live in them. They wanted Him to change them. Yet the grip of the world seemed unchallengeable in their lives.

I did all I could to instruct them, for they were already evangelical Christians. That is to say, they *believed* everything you and I believe: God is Three and One — Father, Son and Holy Spirit; Jesus is fully God and fully man; He was born of a virgin and worked miracles; He died so that we could have life; the Bible is God's infallible word; we must personally accept His work on the Cross; we are sinners and cannot save ourselves; and we must grow in grace and purity. Many of them had prayed to receive the baptism of the Holy Spirit and some of them spoke in tongues. And they prayed desperately to God and found so much joy in our Bible studies.

But the world still claimed them.

Their lives were almost unchanged. What was I doing wrong? Suddenly what James had to say about the doctrines of demons took on a new light. When James defined the doctrine of demons, he pointed out that they believe the truth just as we do. They believe in one God. By implication, they also believe that Jesus is God, that the Bible is God's word, that Jesus died for our sins. They believe in the Trinity, and every other tenet of the faith once for all delivered to the saints. So what is the difference between demons and Christians? dead faith and living faith? Doesn't faith save you? Faith which transforms you saves you. Is the other kind really *faith*? Or is it demonic, dead faith?

This was a great dilemma for me. If God has a place reserved in heaven for the first evangelical church of Atlanta, or any other city, He must have room for the sinners of cell-block 500. Is this good news for the inmates in my cell block? Or is it bad news for the evangelicals of American Christianity? It might be bad news if you stop to consider that if the "Christians" of cell block 500 are not saved, then neither are we evangelicals who believe the same doctrines and have learned to accommodate ourselves to *our* level of sin as they accommodate themselves to *their* level of sin.

The comparison between nice suburban evangelical faith — faith which has supported and financed the growth of the Church around the world in this century — and the wasted faith of the average prison Christian is not obvious until you start thinking about the implications of basic doctrines for how we should live when people are killing babies. We all have a way of easing into the good life and fashioning a faith to fit, whether in the urban jungle, or in the suburbs. *These are the doctrines of demons: Transforming truths which fail to transform us.* Rescue is nothing more than orthodox Christianity transforming Christians in the arena of legalized child murder. Fundamental Christian doctrine can transform even something as established as the pro-life movement . . . or the American Church.

Rescue Is Not the Same as Civil Disobedience

There are two unfortunate reasons why many commentators have not seen how orthodox Christianity — the Cross — defines Rescue. The first is their general knowledge of Gandhi, Thoreau, and King. They suppose that little more can be learned in the area of nonviolent civil disobedience. And certainly not from this unlettered rabble of Rescuers. Their general knowledge gives them a false sense of knowing the issues at stake. As a result, they feel little need to glean facts first hand. They content themselves with fitting the few facts they do encounter into their preconceived categories.

The second reason these commentators fail to see the heart

of what we do is simply, I fear, because they do not want to. Such knowledge is too costly; they fear the slippery slope. Pro-life literature is full of the slippery slope argument: first they kill the unborn; then the new-born "defectives;" then the old and infirm; then finally the "useless parasites" whose beliefs do not square with the state's. But this is not the slippery slope which most Christians fear. We fear the simple assertion: *"Abortion kills children."* Once you start down that slope, where will you end? To understand Rescue is to listen with God to that silent scream — scream, after scream, after scream, after scream — and not stop listening. There has yet to be a critique of Rescue which has the courage to look these children in the eye. Read them. Each critique focuses on questions of "Marxist revolution," "effective long-range strategy," and "civil disobedience." They are monumental efforts to justify why it is right to cooperate with and protect baby-killers . . . anything to keep the screams of today's children out of mind and heart.

That simple assertion, *"Abortion kills children,"* continually draws all those with the courage to listen to press beyond the surface of philosophical banter thrown up by the critics. Yet we are afraid of where it might lead if we take even the simplest steps to act as if someone needs our help. That road is too dangerous; it is best left alone. It is this general fear which gives the critics credibility. It is certainly not their heartless, irrational, and hysterical arguments.

They say Rescue relies on Marxist tactics? Accusing Christians of destabilizing society because they obey God rather than men is not a new strategy. Demetrius the silversmith of Acts 19 originated this hysterical attack. "These Christians are trying to turn the world upside down!" was a slogan he would be comfortable with. The only thing new in today's accusation against Rescue is to attribute saving a baby's life to Marx. While it is true that some leaders of Operation Rescue valued Rescues for creating the tension in society which can change the law, that is scarcely the same as Marxism which values confusion so as to seize power. When you obey *men* rather than God, in time either God or the *men whom you obey* will prevail. Where godless, lawless men prevail, Christianity is scheduled for destruction. The reign of Man in Marxist countries, and the growing control by secular humanism in the West, are examples of this.[1] On the other hand, when you obey *God* rather than men, you may lose your life while for a season men's lawlessness prevails, but in time, you will transform the laws, customs, and civilizations of men to first accommodate and finally to honor and reflect God's way as it is lived out in His people. Transformation through godly obedience is scarcely comparable to seizing power through revolutionary destabilization. Godly obedience is no threat to righteous order. If a grain of wheat falls to the ground and dies, then it will not abide alone. This is a Biblical principle which applies to weeds also. This is hardly Marxism, though it is the Biblically expounded mechanism in creation which many Christians ignore, preferring to go along to get along.

They irrationally say Rescue is not an effective long-range strategy? For some reason, those who argue about the best strategy to overcome legalized abortion never seem to think that laying down your life is a reasonable strategy. But what is wrong with this long-range strategy: "We fifty million Christians in America would rather rot in jail and see our houses and churches seized for the next 100 years than possess them at the expense of cooperating in any way with child-killing"? If you say this is impossible, then we are lost. If we do not get at least fifty million people convinced that life is this important, then we will never pass a lasting law which will make life safe in the womb or anywhere else — laws don't change hearts, hearts change laws. There must be someone or some group who will show us what this heart change is. Someone who will say: "I would rather spend the rest of my life in jail than cooperate with child-killing." Historically it has been Christians who have led the way with individual, sacrificial obedience as their long-range strategy, teaching tool, political motivator, and Gospel witness.

---

[1] When Christians obey God rather than man, they are identifiably Christian. Godless laws can destroy them by wiping them out physically. A more thorough form of destruction, however, is when Christians accommodate themselves to godless laws. Though they are spared physical destruction, they undergo a no less radical spiritual destruction which in time accomplishes the same purpose. The only difference between the two forms of destruction is that in one, Christians are destroyed by godless men for refusing to live by their godless laws and way of life. In the other, "Christians" are destroyed by God for their cooperation in godlessness.

They heartlessly say Rescue is merely civil disobedience? Framing the issue in terms of civil disobedience and protest is a very convenient and scholarly way to keep our eyes on an "issue" instead of on God and the children. But it constructs a straw man. Rescue theory does bear the resemblance of a second cousin to civil disobedience theory, though it is not reducible to it, much as Jesus' ministry, though having points in common with mass evangelism and seminar ministries, is not reducible to these modern categories. The things we do are shaped by very different concerns:

1) *Lawbreaking* — We do not break man's law in order to make a point, show our resolve, or even protest the injustice of the law we broke. *At the outset we contend that because we saved a life we have not broken even man's laws.* The value of human life still precedes mere property in American law. Nevertheless, since the police and courts value property more than life in this matter, they charge us with lawbreaking. Even if we grant their warped perspective and call it "breaking a law," *we only "break man's law" at those points where to fail to break it will make us accomplices of the abortionist's murder.* Getting arrested does indeed make a point and show resolve, but this is not even close to the heart of Rescue.[2]

2) *Protest* — People are forever calling Rescues "protests." To do this displays wilful ignorance of the most fundamental facts. Traditional civil disobedience advocates lawbreaking as a means of protesting injustice. For instance, if you were *protesting* an unsafe pool in which a man was drowning, you might shout, "I hate drowning!" or, "It's immoral to permit pools with no lifeguards!" You might even write your congressman, picket offending pools, scream, "Murderer!" at their owners, or drain the pools at night. But if you would stop *this* man from drowning, you would not shout, you would bring him to land. You would do so despite any "No TRESPASSING" signs that were posted to keep anti-poolians like you off the property. That is Rescue.

---

[2] For instance, I have led about 2,000 people in 8 different Rescues *out of* arrest situations as soon as we knew that children's lives were no longer in danger that day.

Protest is important, but for Rescue it is only incidental. We could use civil disobedience to *protest* abortion in many ways. We could tie up city blocks at rush hour; shut down businesses; picket on private property; even sit-in at city hall. All of these would be classic acts of civil disobedience. But for what has come to be called "Rescue," neither Gandhi nor Thoreau tell us where to go or what to do. We are compelled to follow the footsteps of Jesus to the Cross. Rescue goes far beyond promoting the idea that abortion is wrong — which is the goal of a protest, even a civil disobedience protest. You can agree with a protester and have it cost you nothing. Rescue shapes an activity which says, "To *permit* abortion is wrong." You cannot afford to even agree with a Rescuer. It might cost you everything.

The Two Goals of Rescue

There are, then, two goals of Rescue. The first and controlling goal is that of saving an innocent life. The second, is to do so in a way that conforms our message and method to the principles of the Cross, thereby bringing lasting heart-change to our Church and society.

Goal #1: Saving Life: Every symbolic and tactical point in a Rescue and its aftermath in courts, jails, and politics, flows out of this central concern. The Rescuer shapes everything he does by his desire to quit protecting child-killing himself and to make it impossible for courts and politicians to protect the killing. He goes to the doors of the abortion factories, and personally closes them. In court he becomes a witness to proclaim the God whom he serves at any penalty, and to defend not himself, but the children whose lives he has protected.

Goal #2: Symbolic clarity which speaks to the hearts of men and the standards of society. To go beyond mere revolution and surface political/legal change, Rescuers realize that every action must carry a heart-changing message. This symbolic dimension of Rescue is defined by the Cross of our Lord. When innocent lives are threatened by the blood-lust of an entire society — fueled by the apathy of its churches — it is not enough just to save that life. We must inspire people to become life savers as Jesus Himself laid out the pattern to transform the world.

Rescuers stay up all night agonizing over the smallest details of their tactics, concerned for the message and symbol they will convey to the watching world. The message, in a nutshell, is: "The Church stands *with* the helpless children, *against* their killers, and *against* whoever seeks to forcibly protect their killers." This message preached by the Cross is the necessary heart of true social change — good law requires the fertile soil of hearts prepared to live and die according to it. As Christians become that rich seed-bed of practical righteousness, child-killing will become illegal from within our system as it becomes intolerable to our lives. As Screwtape was heard commenting to his nephew Wormwood the other day, "If the Church keeps protecting the little ones, then the government might as well change the law to make abortion illegal, because the Christians won't let our doctors sacrifice to us any more anyway."

We may add these two goals to the last chapter's diagram by adding two rings. The inner ring is the primary goal of saving a helpless, innocent life. The outer ring is how we focus and describe our actions. The triangle is still Rescue.

Principle #1:
ATONEMENT
Physical
Intervention

Goal #2

Principle #3:
INCARNATION
Identification

**Goal #1
Save
Lives**

Change Hearts

Principle #2:
SUBMISSION
Harmlessness

There is, however, more that we can do to this diagram to illustrate how the principles of the Cross define Rescue. These three principles of the Cross establish the three boundaries of each Rescue tactic. If you follow any one or two principles to its extreme, you are not taking the "next logical step" of Rescue. Rather you are stepping out of the realm of one clearly defined activity — Rescue — into the realm of some other activity. Press *harmlessness* to its extreme, and you do nothing. Press *identification with the child*, and you have self-immolation. Press *intervention* and you have bombing. Put them all together and you have none of these. You have Rescue.

BASIC PRINCIPLES *vs* EXTREME CONCLUSIONS

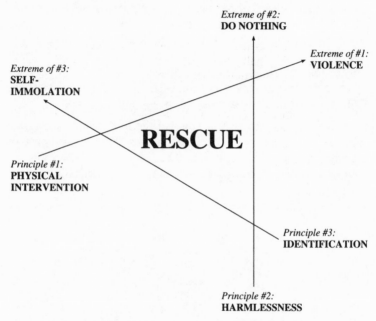

Extreme of #2:
DO NOTHING

Extreme of #1:
VIOLENCE

Extreme of #3:
**SELF-
IMMOLATION**

RESCUE

Principle #1:
**PHYSICAL
INTERVENTION**

Principle #3:
IDENTIFICATION

Principle #2:
HARMLESSNESS

This diagram should help make clear how most arguments against Rescue rest on a complete redefinition of Rescue, in terms of whatever extreme is convenient for the critic.

What Rescue Does Lead To

If you can understand the internal dynamic of Rescue, then you can see that determining what Rescue will lead to — or our next logical step — is not a simplistic matter of taking one principle to its extreme. If Rescue leads to anything, it would be as soon to politics, or to doing nothing, as to bombing.

With the rise of Rescue, death camp bombings stopped

almost completely.[3]   With Rescue's apparent demise as a publicly perceived force, the bombers will no doubt return along with the politicians. Will Rescue lead to these bombings? No. If anything leads to bombing, it is the absence of a clear, sacrificial call to live and die a Christian. This vacuum leads to every other "solution" — from politics and Jericho marches, to bombings. For most of us, the pearl of great price is not worth the cost of what we would have to sell to buy it and so we try solutions less costly to ourselves.

There is no further "step" outside of Rescue to which Rescue's internal dynamic leads. The only real question will be, "Will the world finally teach the Church that it is wrong to try to save a baby from murder? Is saving life a way of life, or is it just another strategy to try, and then return to the good life?"

What Rescue does lead to, is the challenge to free ourselves from those things which become idols in our lives. We cannot free ourselves from every responsibility — like marriage and supporting a family — nor would we suggest doing so. But we can make every responsibility a reflection and springboard to laying down our lives. We can begin to take steps today so that within a year or two we will be free to do more. We can begin to prepare ourselves, our possessions, our families, and our churches to do those things that might cause us to forfeit everything we, like the pagans, cling to in this life. *The tragedy is not that so few Christians are ready to sit-in. The tragedy is that so few Christians are free to leave everything behind to follow their Lord no matter what the issue might be.*[4]

---

[3] Rescue is seldom credited with the dramatic increased pro-life activity of every sort since 1988. And yet Rescue is accused of leading to bombing though bombing dropped dramatically after 1988. Why are Rescue critics so willing to use any piece of shoddy thinking to stone Rescue? The reason lies not in logic, reason, or facts. It lies in a deeper fear which lurks in all of us. See Chapter 7, under "This Present Darkness." (p 94)

[4] Since most of the Church thinks that only radical "spiritual" callings like jungle Bible translation, or torture in the Gulag, require dying to yourself, I want to stress that it is not just Rescue which I want added to the list, but running your business and darning your socks. In fact, I want to de-radicalize the whole notion of being "spiritual," whether in the Gulag or in front of an abortion clinic. A clear example of what I am talking about is a janitorial franchise called *Environment Control*, for whom I worked for

This must change. We cannot be free from responsibilities, but we can keep our responsibilities from being our excuses to let the children die, to let the inner city die, to let the nations die, to let our churches become the tombs of the faith. We must not let our legitimate responsibilities become illegitimate idols preventing our whole-hearted obedience to God — preventing our becoming Rescuers in any arena.

Rescue will clarify in people's minds the ongoing historic ministry of the Church. Saving a baby's life does not nullify other pro-life activities; it fulfills them. It provides them teeth and final credibility. On the Cross Jesus did not nullify his preaching and healing ministry, nor did He do away with the law of righteousness — rather He fulfilled them. We need to bring Rescue into the full ministry of churches so that they no longer fear what men can do to their tax status and property. There is only one way to communicate this effectively, and that will never be in books like this, but in our lives. How does anyone looking at your life know that you refuse to compromise with evil? The same way he tells the difference between your faith and the faith of those in cell block 500.

The Ministry of the Church

Whether saving a life, protecting a reputation, feeding the hungry, or bringing the Good News of the Most High God to souls bent on destruction — Rescue is a ministry of the Church. It requires God's salvation to transform hearts so that they can act like Christ in prophetic, priestly, and kingly ministry.

Sometimes, acting like Christ gets a Christian thrown in jail for nothing more than following Christ's prophetic, priestly, and

---

five years prior to the launching of Operation Rescue. Daryl Kraft, the franchisor, applied to the humblest of businesses all of the principles which sound so radical when we apply them to legalized abortion. They are radical only because people like Daryl are not commonplace in the Church. If he were, we would not have abortion on demand. Someday to make this point I would love to write a book, *The Cross and the Toilet*. In God's kingdom, what makes us radically spiritual is not how far we distance ourselves from the world, but how far we transform *all* things in creation into the image of what He intended, from bathroom to board room, from personal ethics to societal norms, from the standards of self-discipline to the laws of a nation.

kingly pattern in some arena of life. *Whenever it is made illegal to act like Christ, then it is only by risking trial and jail that the Christian can give the Church an opportunity in that particular arena to minister to the world in its unique role as prophet, priest, and king.* The task of the Church is to call forth, train, lay hands on, send out, and support people who will obey God, whether it is legal or illegal to do so. When we ordain such missionaries to the people in the womb, we are ordaining men and women who will refuse to compromise with whatever worldly principle, law, or judge is sending Christians to jail for obeying God.[5] Though the Church is not physically in prison with them, these imprisoned Christians give the whole Church the unique opportunity to become:

1) **Prophetic** — *Paying any price to stand in solidarity with the truth as we interpose ourselves between killer and victim or between judge and Rescuer*: The Christian by rescuing regardless of cost, and the Church by standing with him and defending its own, speaks a clear message to the legal-political systems of this age: "Let my people go, that they may serve Me!" Society cannot receive God's blessing by persecuting the righteous, nor can the Church by ignoring their persecution and cooperating with their destruction.

---

[5] As pointed out on page 29, both state and federal law permit citizens to rescue innocent children from the premeditated destruction of their life. Yet these same laws are almost universally interpreted by judges, prosecutors, and policemen as forbidding us to Rescue these children. Throughout this book, when I call Rescue "illegal" I am only pragmatically referring to the interpretation of these misdirected lawmen. We have broken neither the letter nor spirit of America's laws in any Rescue — there is no statute, constitutional clause, or Supreme court decision which makes it illegal to for a citizen to protect the life of a child in the womb. In time, the interpretation of judges will return to the sanity of the our statutes and the Constitution as they now stand. How long this takes is entirely up to you.

So effective is the argument for the *legality* of Rescue that we have rarely been permitted by the courts to present it, though it would only take ten to thirty minutes of testimony and evidence to do so. So powerful is this evidence that where it has been permitted we have either been acquitted or we have been found guilty but not punished. Knowing this, courts suppress it before the trials begin. If you have never been to one of these trials, I am sure you doubt this. The most often repeated words of anyone who for the first time hears what these courts do is, "They can't do that . . . can they?"

2) **Priestly** — *Interposing ourselves harmlessly*: The Christian, by his harmlessness at the clinic and helplessness in jail, intervenes for the children. In union with the churches who minister through him, he expresses our ministry of priestly interposition on the children's behalf.

3) **Kingly** — *Interposing ourselves physically on behalf of others*: The Church does not establish God's law by coercive decree, but by its example of suffering and service. By sending forth and standing with people who intervene for the children, the whole Church becomes a living example of the law of love. In love of God they serve Him at any cost. In love of society, they suffer by standing in the path of its sinful destruction of others and itself. In love of the little ones, they stand in their place. As our King led through suffering service, we do too: we suffer rather than accept either the extreme of striking back at society, or the extreme of leaving society to its own devices. The Church by standing with the Rescuers — its direct representatives — makes its ministry of healing compassion known by personally paying the price to establish justice. The Christian stands for justice even if that means the seizing of his house and sanctuary, or the inconvenient discipline of a daily phone call to hold a rebel-judge accountable to the King. *If we cannot express our kingly office as Christ did, on a cross, then we are not fit to change any law or seize political power through lobbying and voter registration. We serve God even if that means jail. As God sees fit, we let whatever authority He gives us come to us there rather than lust after it in our political caucuses. The power to rule is the power to serve.*

It would be a shame if the cost of the Cross as expressed in Rescue would cause the Church to draw back from this unique opportunity to stand in the gap either personally, or through direct support of our missionaries who stand there as much for us as for the nameless little ones.

Chapter 4

RESCUE AND THE CHRISTIAN LIFE

Yes, But Is it Normal?

While attending Seminary in Philadelphia, I just knew that some day the doors of the library would burst open and one of the overworked students would come leaping out shouting at the top of his lungs, with a mad gleam in his eye, "There *is* a God! There *is* a God! He exists, and He fits in with *my* system!" When I first developed the outline of what a Rescue is in its Biblical and historical context, I was immediately suspicious that I had fulfilled my own expectations. Was I guilty of special pleading? Had I simply found a convenient way to justify an activity? One way to test this is to see if these principles of the Cross are actually played out in the general ebb and flow of Christian living. Do other aspects of a normal Christian life also follow this pattern as an ideal? After all, taking up the Cross is not a special call for a few super-Christians. Jesus made it the standard measure of any follower: "If *any*one would be My disciple, let him take up his cross and follow Me." This chapter will examine the broader application of the principles of the Cross — Rescue — to the Christian life.

Yo! Rev! What You Know 'bout Satisfyin' Wimmin?

The inmates in Fulton County Jail live in a world which has no up or down, no right or wrong, beyond the motto: "Don't get caught." To them the very idea of marriage or fidelity is impossible, unthinkable, unbearable. How then, could the simple values of the Scripture reach them? If they could not understand faithfulness in respect to marriage, is it any surprise that they were so untrustworthy in the rest of their lives?

One day, I was writing letters in the common room and the argument raging around me that morning was between which sexual practices would satisfy women the best. As the argument came to a stalemate — so to speak — one of the wags noticed I was there and said, "Yo! Rev! What you know 'bout satisfyin' wimmin?"

Without looking up, I answered, "Probably more than the rest of you put together, listening to how you all talk so big."

"Whooo Weeeeee!" They began to hoot and holler. "The Rev dun an' become a expert on sex!" So I turned back to writing my letter.

Another cackled, "He probbly does know more'n you, Red!"

"It ain't hard to know more'n Red!"

"That what Trina tells me anyhow,"

"You goin' down playuh! Hard!" chimed in three at once.

As the clamor died down, he had to accept my challenge. "What you mean?" he asked. "I mean, you the Reverend and everything, and you say you know more'n the rest of us?"

"Well, I'll say this, none of you in this room can keep a woman satisfied for 14 years and have her still coming back for more." There was silence, so I went on, "Anybody has what it takes to keep a woman happy for a day or two, but from the sound of it, you can't keep it up much longer than that. You want the real thing? You just keep the same girl satisfied for 14 years, and you'll find out it takes a whole lot more than what you all are talking about. Come back in ten or fifteen years and then let's talk about who can satisfy who."

Yo! Church! What You Know 'bout Satisfyin' God?

The world is an expert on satisfying its gods and stops from time to time to mock the Church with, "Yo! Church! What you know 'bout satisfyin' God?" But how can the Church answer? We know that only the Cross of Jesus Christ satisfied God's justice. We know that only taking up His Cross will satisfy God's ethical requirements for our daily life, conforming us to the image of His Son — "If any man would be My disciple . . ." Yet half the Church has the shallow, faddish, bless-me fire insurance which lures converts by mimicking the world's way of satisfying its trendy gods; while the other half has a stable relationship to God which is like a marriage that died years ago, though the outward forms of fidelity remain "for the children's sake." In other words, the bride of Christ is either jumping from lover to lover for an exciting "faith," or after fifteen years of faithful external observance it is rather bored with God and "not coming back for more."

Much of the American Church today is incapable of understanding what any solution to abortion will require, because we are no more capable of committing ourselves to a lifetime of faithful, sacrificial obedience to God than my congregation in Fulton County Jail was capable of understanding a lifetime of faithful commitment in marriage. Therefore, the fruit of such faithfulness seems like a mirage. Christians given to formality only seem to respect those who lose everything for Jesus Christ as long as those who have done so are safely dead — preferably for centuries. Yet in the land of the fad, fast-growing churches have the opposite problem. They are under intense pressure to keep Christianity exciting and fun — as if the message of the Cross was only for the early Church. It has almost become a point of dogma that Church growth depends on finding people who are socially "just like us" and building homogenous groups. Other exciting, growing churches tell us that God's Spirit moves in waves: the Latter Rain Movement, then the Charismatic Movement, then the Shepherding Movement, then the Rescue Movement and tomorrow who knows what other movement. My point is not that God is not doing something in these movements, but that a mark of God's work is that He establishes it — He does not come and go with some ever-changing program to keep up our interest and excitement while we stay confined in safe ghettos. Isn't it time we start being satisfied by *God*? Isn't it time we get beyond reducing God's abiding work to the level of America's homophile designer gods and their latest fads?

God has been faithfully patient for thousands of years working His plan, the climax of which was a cross. He rescued us and calls us to become Rescuers with Him, having lives which exhibit that same Cross. There are no cheap or simple solutions to abortion, certainly no purely political and educational solutions. This is because abortion itself is not a problem to be solved, but a solution in its own right — a very costly solution, as all murder is costly. Think about it: All abortions kill an innocent person for one of two reasons — either the victim is an innocent witness to the sin of his parents and so must be silenced, or the victim will cost too much to love and care for.

Any solution that hopes to replace the abortion solution must be equally costly. Only the Cross is costly enough.

It is time to stop deceiving Christians by telling them, *"All we are asking you to do is write a letter, or come to this picket, or do this 'rescue' with us."* The children ask considerably more. The God who hears them demands considerably more. Creation groans, longing for considerably more. The God who hears their cry, will do considerably more — either with us, or to us.

The sum of this book is that Rescue is Christianity and Christianity is Rescue. Joshua — Yeshua — Jesus — Savior — Rescuer. Have no other gods before Me. Love God with all your heart, soul, mind, and strength. Love your neighbor as yourself. Have the mind of Christ who became a servant. Be not conformed to this world but be transformed. If you love Me you will keep My commandments. Make disciples of all nations and teach them to obey whatsoever I have commanded you. If any man would be My disciple, let him take up his cross and follow Me. Friendship with the world is enmity with God. These things are so common to all Christians that there is no need to footnote them. They are not taken out of context. They are all Rescue passages pure and simple. They are the core passages for understanding Christian living because Christian living is a commitment to be a Rescuer until God calls us home, not a commitment to drift, or to surf the faddish waves of His Spirit until the next wave comes in.

What Makes a "Sit-in" a Biblical Rescue?

To some Operation Rescue appeared to be merely another fad because we failed to define abortion sit-ins in terms of our Biblical and historic faith and practice. Although it was a profound expression of that faith, on the surface it looked like just a rerun of 1960's activism. We discovered that a long haul cannot depend on a fad. It must draw from the never-failing wellsprings which water every other part of our Christian life.

Of all the pro-life activities directed at protecting the children whose mothers turn down every persuasive argument and offer of help and go into the death camps, Operation Rescue is the most patterned after the Cross. It is not a way-station on the continuum between violence and non-violence. It is not a technique of social protest we borrowed from Gandhi and Thoreau. In fact, to the extent that Gandhi and Thoreau have credibility, they borrow it from the principles of Rescue which our Lord laid down. Rescue at an abortion death camp is not even the most strenuous or costly thing someone could do. We do it because, of everything within our power to do, sitting between killer and victim is more like what Christ did on the Cross than it is like any other type of activity. A sit-in has more to do with the heart and soul of our faith than it does with abstract questions of civil disobedience, social tension, and creating political change. Rescue is not civil disobedience; it is godly obedience.

I am not against political action, blowing up clinics, crisis pregnancy centers, taking an unwed mother into your home, and sidewalk counseling day in and day out. All of these activities, in their own way, have as their goal protecting children from the psychopathic, child-molesting, serial killers whom the law protects. But, which one of them fulfills all three aspects of the Cross at once for the child whose mother has turned down every other appeal and is walking through the door of the death chamber? Only sit-ins as they have been modified and developed by Operation Rescue, bringing together 15 years of intervention experience in front of abortion death chambers, with 4,000 years of Biblical experience, doctrine, and church history.

I am not saying that the sit-in itself is required. My point is that giving yourself utterly in this three-fold way is required. So far, I have only seen the sit-in fulfill this form for the 4,500 children a day whose mothers refuse *all* other appeals.

This is how sit-ins become Rescue — they are simply an expression of a normal Christian way of life. What else would a Christian do? If you can think of a better way to protect an innocent, helpless, trusting life, then do it. I am not arguing for sit-ins as such. I have simply been unable to think of an alternative which will stop the murder, save the victim, and not hurt anyone or anything in the process. If protecting a child by passively keeping his killer away from him seems odd, it is not the Rescue which is out of order, it is the rest of our lives.

Why We Do Not See Sit-ins in the Bible

The Bible does not have much in it dealing with how to change society through movements of social activism, and sit-ins have been used historically as just that. *But what if sitting-in is not primarily used for protest, but for the defense of life?* This is *the* question which no critic of Rescue has dealt with. What if we no longer use the sit-in as a tool for exposing evil (its traditional use)? What if instead we employ it to protect those against whom some evil thing is intended? The Bible says a great deal about intervening to protect the innocent. Most of the Biblical interventions were a bit more violent. Yet, will God be upset if our intervention takes the nonviolent form of a group of people standing between a killer and his victim, regardless of how often a sit-in has been put to other purposes?

The reason we see little social activism in the Bible is because the Bible focuses on more direct means of bringing social change. These revolve for the most part around people who personally went about the business of obeying God regardless of the cost, and in time the laws fell into line, or God brought down the government, or they were killed for obeying God. Then on the Cross, our Lord showed us how to serve, how to be pastors, missionaries, housewives, husbands, workers, children, parents, masters, servants. "This is how you bring social change." says the Cross, "Be a Rescuer in every area of life — take up your cross, deny yourself, and follow Me."

As Christians see that stopping their cooperation with child murder is no longer good press, will they turn to other things? Will we cling to the straw man of "the futility of protest," or "the wrongness of Marxist tactics for creating social tension?" Or, will we finally decide that it is worthwhile for *someone* to lose his life in the effort to intervene for the helpless, in a way which is harmless (non-revolutionary) and identifies him with them so thoroughly that for the world to destroy the child it must destroy the Christian first?

Rescue is not a strategy. It is how we live our lives as Christians. The underground railroad was not a strategy to abolish the "slavery issue." It is what the serious Christian did to abolish slavery for this slave, then that slave, and then the next slave. They did not look at slavery as an "issue." They looked at the slave personally: young Tom whom they sold away from his wife Anne and three small children Jeneane, Billy, and Anne-Marie. They saw slavery, not as some vague social evil, but as *people* in bondage. Therefore they helped *people* escape bondage. They knew that ultimately, until God healed the warping of the soul which slavery effected in slave holder, slave, and bystander alike, there would be no satisfactory solution. But they did not use this huge vague philosophical/ spiritual reality to justify not doing what they could to end slavery. Instead they focused on what *they could do:* personally free as many slaves as they could. What kind of a solution was that? What kind of strategy? It was not a strategy at all. If slavery lasted another hundred years, their grandchildren would have kept on fighting it, one freed slave at a time. The underground railroad was not primarily a strategy, it was a way of life — it was Rescue.

For all the talk I have heard about the Civil Rights Movement being similar to Rescue, I have never been able to see many similarities, with one exception. Martin Luther King, Jr., made a crucial shift in the movement which had been going nowhere for about 60 years. Because of his shift, the more respectable main-stream black groups, like the NAACP, resented his uppity Southern Christian Leadership Conference. What did he do? He decided that instead of acting like a second-class citizen and begging to be given first class-rights, he would act like a first-class citizen, assume those rights, and let others prove that he was not human enough to deserve them. He would drink out of the first-class citizen's water fountain and use his toilets. He would eat in his restaurants, buy shoes in the front of the store, and ride in the front of a bus — or not at all. This "disrespectful" approach horrified the establishment civil rights groups even more than it horrified the white racists, because the backlash would (and did) hurt them all — much as the Israelites suffered when Moses refused to take a "No" from Pharaoh. But it is hard to argue against his logic even had he failed as so many failed before him. His logic was simple: If even *you* are not going to act like a normal citizen where *your* rights as a citizen are at stake, then why should anyone else think that you deserve to be treated like a citizen?

In the same way, if the Christians, who claim that the people in the womb are their equal, do not treat them as their equal, why should anyone else treat people in the womb with full equality — especially someone who does *not* think they are equal? Rescue breaks with begging for the recognition of their right to life. We simply recognize it, act on it, and let the chips fall wherever God has ordained them to fall. *We will treat the unborn as first-class citizens.* This will become the keystone of all other efforts for their enfranchisement and constitutional protection. As a strategy? No! Because, whether people in the womb ever gain constitutional protection in our lifetime or not, we throw in our lot with the helpless because it is the Christian way. The Constitution, after all, can protect only those whom the people have a will to protect. Ask any black man. Ask any Japanese American. Ask any unborn American being carried to the abortionist for his final check-up — our nation's own Final Solution to the Jewish (or any other) pregnancy problem.

We do not see sit-ins in the Bible, but we do see people intervening to rescue others in many ways: from assassination, to helping spies, to midwives lying and delivering children, to intimidating bad rulers (Saul, the Pharisees, and Herod, for example) who often for a time restrained their legal but evil intentions "for fear of the people." Above all, what sets the pattern for all of us today is God rescuing His people on the Cross. Then God reaches through His people — through the power of their testimony, the blood of the Lamb, and that they do not love their lives unto death — to rescue the world.

Rescue: the Pattern of Christian Ministry

If God rescued the world through His Cross, then we should expect to find the pattern of His Rescue to be seen, not only in Operation Rescue, but in every other sort of Christian ministry. The basis of world missions and home missions is that Christians work together to send a missionary to live with and minister directly to those who need the Gospel — to physically intervene. They become a part of the lives of the people to whom they minister — they identify with the person to whom they go with the Gospel. When they go, they share the risks of disease, of losing their families, and in some cases they even risk being killed.[1] All the weapons of spiritual warfare will not convert one pygmy if they are not backing up a Christian who is working with pygmies. The Christian in the field gives the rest of the Church a tangible point to reach through to others who would not otherwise hear or see the Gospel. This is Rescue: the Church banding together to support its members who are the living extensions of Christian love and witness.

Inner-city ministry, or any other home ministry, also shows this pattern. While it is good to take a youth group into the city to work on someone's roof, street-preach, or witness in the bars, the foundation for this is laid by men and women who rent a flat in the ghetto and live with the rats, roaches, and life-threatening crime that mark our urban crisis. They put their lives and their children's lives on the line. They are Rescuers. They understand spiritual warfare. They understand the hell that earth becomes wherever men do not respect God's standards. They know where to minister — where it is most like hell. There they begin to make a difference just by living by the self-sacrificing standards of the Gospel. It really is Good News. They physically intervene in the lives of those around them. They are harmless to their neighbors — they do not build a personal power base or kingdom. They voluntarily suffer the degradation, humiliation, and powerlessness of those to whom they minister. They Rescue.

When I think of an effective pastor, who bears his people's burdens, I think of my brother, a Presbyterian minister in middle Tennessee. He knows his people's circumstances intimately and he will suffer whatever he must to see them built up in their faith and practice of godliness. No one is too insignificant for him, and no one too great. He is far more than the man you keep around to bless various occasions of state, like the high school

---

[1] My Father, Kenneth J. Foreman, Jr., was held prisoner by the Chinese Communists. Though he was not martyred, some of those he ministered to were. Jim Elliot was murdered by Auca Indians in South America. The martyr is not unusual in the history of missions. They experience what all missionaries risk. When people ask what the principles of the Missionaries to the Preborn are, we tell them first to read the biographies of great missionaries like William Carey, C.T. Studd, Hudson Taylor, and Paul. Read especially, *By their Blood*, by James and Marti Hefley; Baker.

football game, or the pot-luck supper. In his ministry you can see the Cross made plain. He is physically with his flock in good times and bad. He is harmless, not grasping after wealth, prestige, or engaged in pulpit power plays. These same characteristics mark all real pastors, regardless of where their church is, or its resources — men like Jim Pinto in urban Birmingham, Alabama, Dan Hall in the suburbs of Jackson, Mississippi, Al Howard in the pits of Long Beach, California. These shepherds are always laying down their lives for the sheep. This is the pattern of Rescue. The good shepherd is a Rescuer.

Rescue: the Pattern of A Marriage

Many people will tell you that heavy involvement in Operation Rescue can take a toll on your marriage. While this is generally true of all heavy commitments, not just Rescue, it is also true that marriages today are quite fragile. In America we have set a track record in our marriages of being unfaithful and undependable — not necessarily in big ways, but certainly in all the small petty ones. We do not have Biblical marriages.[2] We have good American marriages. Even where we are sexually faithful and work hard at our careers, you cannot find the Cross in many marriages. When you do, you notice something different about that couple.

Operation Rescue was one of the best things which could have happened to Anne's and my marriage. Starting years before I had ever heard of Randy Terry, I realized that if Anne and I were ever to be Biblically one, I was going to have to die to myself. What I discovered years later is that this is not a unique requirement for marriage; it is the general pattern of the Christian life. It is Rescue.

The principles which prepared me to have a part in Operation Rescue leadership were hammered out in my marriage years before I ever thought about abortion. In 1981 I was graduating from seminary, looking for my first church. Anne and I had two children and a marriage which was about as empty

---

[2] A shame of the Church today is that our families are so weak that a marriage counselor can make a good living ministering exclusively to Christian couples!

as one could be. Not bad, just empty. We had very little in common. I did things to make her feel small and insecure. She did things to make me feel useless. Not big things, just consistent, thoughtless, small-time selfishness on each of our parts, built up over the years. Nothing to lead us to a life-changing crisis. Nothing to apologize for and start afresh.

I realized that both of us had the ideal in mind of the perfect husband and wife. Yet, we were both disappointed, in ourselves and each other. Why were finances always an argument? Why were so many things a struggle? Why didn't she love me the way I loved her? Why couldn't I love her the way *she* wanted to be loved? Why couldn't we work together instead of picking away at each other — especially in front of people? Why couldn't we agree on how to discipline the kids? Why couldn't we resist making small, publicly-embarrassing comments?

The answer that came to me was so simple. It was in Ephesians 5:25, "Husbands, love your wives as Christ loved the Church and gave Himself for her that He might sanctify her and cleanse her . . . that He might present her to Himself a glorious Church." Here was the pattern of the Cross in marriage. I was to lay down my life for Anne in a way that makes her glorious. As Proverbs 31 says, "Let her own works praise her in the gate." But how? How could I free her to shine in all her glory?

I realized I had to become *her* servant. I had to make *her* look good. I must decrease but she must increase. Until 1981, I approached the problems in our marriage much the same way the pro-life movement has approached abortion. I believed that there were no problems that a good, long, heart-to-heart talk could not unravel — the education solution to marriage. If nothing else, I figured that I could always just take authority and assume my rightful place as head of the family — the political solution. But unfortunately, my track record of five years of marriage — like the Church's nineteen-year track record on abortion — said it all, robbing me of all authority in my family. I could not sit down with Anne and say, "I'll be different. I'm really going to make you the most important woman in the world. In time you will trust me because you know that on this earth you are my highest priority." I had to say it with my life for as many years as my life had been telling her the opposite.

I began. I picked several small things I would begin to do to serve her and communicate my love, respect, and support to her. Each of these exhibited the pattern of the Cross in three ways: 1) Intervening physically for her where *she* needed and wanted it instead of at *my* convenience; 2) Never using anything to get one up on her or to compete with her; 3) Doing things for her which society considers ignoble, because in Christ nothing that is not sinful is worthless.

These were small ways where I knew I could be consistent — consistency being a higher priority than flashy success. I was sick of big promises and hype. What I did is not that important. What was important is this: I would be utterly consistent; I would never point out what I was doing so she would "know what a great husband I was;" and most of all, I figured it took five years to dig this hole and so I would give my plan as many years before I even began to look for fruit.

What was the result? Even these puny, faltering steps began to bear fruit. We began to become a family prepared to give its life for Christ. Rescue became my family's way of life, long before we ever sat-in at an abortion death camp.

We went into full time pro-life work with no visible means of support. We have had to sell our home. We have not had a steady place to live since then. We have five children. I have led over 120 Rescues. I have spent months in jail. There is no source of income except from people who decide to send checks to Anne. Because of lawsuits by the death-providers I cannot earn any money that will not be garnisheed or seized. We have spent years on the road as a family. Yet all of these things have strengthened rather than destroyed our marriage. Why? Because we are learning how to die to ourselves and for each other. This is the message of the Cross. This is Rescue.

Crossless Marriages, Crossless Churches

Rescue at an abortion clinic is at root no different from Rescue in a Christian marriage. Both stem from imitating the principles of the same Cross. In any good marriage you try to intervene physically for each other in a way that is needed, not just ways which are convenient to the one intervening. You try to be harmless, repenting of the many ways you manipulate each

other to build an edge over the other. You try to identify with
what the other must be going through, rather than put the worst
possible construction on what the other says and does, so as to
justify and nurse your suspicions and resentments. This is the
pattern of the Cross. This is Rescue.

I can hear you now. As you read this you are saying,
"Wait a second! This isn't some fancy pattern. It's just plain old
common sense when it comes to loving your wife. It doesn't
take a theologian to love a wife." I agree fully. The pattern of
the Cross *is* the pattern of the Christian life. *Of course it is
common sense — the Cross is the very definition of common
sense. Why not let it also be our common sense where they
murder children?*

Many families who ran into problems with Operation
Rescue did so because they were not prepared to die to
themselves. Evidence that the common sense of Christianity —
the Cross — is not practiced in many marriages is seen whenever
protecting children threatens the half of the marriage which is
not fully engaged in it. Rescue was a strategy for these couples,
it was not the mark of the Cross over their way of life, and their
marriages suffered. Their children (like their parents) had not
been brought up to take suffering for Jesus Christ for granted,
so they kept wondering why everyone else seemed normal, but
not Mom and Dad. Mom, or Dad, would play on the children's
doubts, and then turn them against the one who was involved in
Rescue. Again and again we heard husbands or wives say, "I
just can't continue because of my wife [or husband]. God has
called me to put my family first. I can't afford a divorce."

Of course they needed to stop rescuing at abortion clinics.
But was the problem Rescue? Or, was it for too many of these
families, that their god was the American Dream? Under normal
circumstances they would never see the inadequacy of their
strange god, but when the Cross poked into their lives, the gap
between the Average Good American Life and losing everything
for Jesus Christ became unbridgeable. Like the rich young
ruler, their face fell. They began to pity themselves and look
for others to join their pity-party.

*Yes, divorce is wrong. But so is the idolatry which has
rotted their marriage, making them unable to devote themselves*

*to the kingdom of God — whether in protecting children from
murder, or any other task which would require them to lose their
life that they might find it. Therefore the kingdom of God, the
Christian home, and individual responsibility, are carefully
redefined so as to exclude any activity which might threaten their
comfort and peace.* Many want to blame Rescue for putting
stress on their marriage (or on any other part of their life where
they have failed and want to blame it on protecting children).
But Rescue merely reveals the cracks which were there, held
together by the illusion of a regular job and peace at any price.

Having said this, it was all too often true that the husband
or wife who rescued was fleeing to the heroic sacrifice of sit-ins
in order to avoid dealing with family problems — and this is as
wrong as the bitterness and resentment of the one who did not
become involved. To both of these sins, the Cross calls out to
let their warfare cease with one another and learn how to trust
and be trust-worthy, to give and to receive. This takes time, but
it can begin now. Such a couple should drop out of abortion
clinic Rescue, but not to return to their old ways of life. Instead
they need to address the idolatry in their marriage which made
them unfit for God's service in any arena, not just the anti-
abortion arena. They must learn to lay down their lives for each
other or they will never get back into the battle, even to so much
as guard the luggage.

Like a marriage grown cold, American Christians have
spent years digging our society into deep trouble. There are no
quick fixes. All we can do is reestablish the kind of track record
which says, "I love you. God loves you. You can depend on
it." Our words to the world, like my words to Anne, lost their
meaning because our society does not see Christians willing to
lay down their lives for *anything* beyond their own peace and
prosperity, much less for murdered babies. What they see is
Christians splitting their churches, destroying their marriages,
chasing the same mirages of success that the world chases —
religion grown quite comfortable, thank-you. This is all they
will see until our lives establish the long-term commitment
necessary to give the Gospel credibility — not respectability, but
credibility. This is true of those parts of our marriage we do not
like, of congregational problems, and problems at work. It is

equally true of grave social evils like abortion, pornography, government education, and the judicial and fiscal crises our country faces. Our solutions will come only as we quietly die to our selfish agendas and live for others by the power of the Spirit — without having the media spotlight what wonderful Christians we are.

For the children being murdered, I know of no strategy for success, only a way of life which strips us down to recognize the crisis we face, the danger we are in, and forces us to take hold with courage of those things which charity, not self-preservation, dictate. We are always trying to tell Jesus what Peter told Him, "No, Lord, the Cross is not for you." We tell Him this in our marriages, our ministries, and our careers. But Jesus rescued us from this perspective when He answered Peter, "Get behind Me, Satan, you are not mindful of the things of God, but the things of men . . . . take up your cross and follow me."[3] When God rescued our marriage, He made possible our good intention to sacrifice for the unborn.

More than any other argument to our husbands, wives, or children, the Rescue marriage says, "I believe you have the same value I do. Therefore, three days, three months, three years, thirty years, of my life laid down to meet whatever need you have, is worth it to restore us to what God intends." More than any other argument to our society and churches, Rescue says, "I believe you have the same value I do, therefore, three days, three months, three years, or thirty years of my life laid down in jail to protect you is worth it to restore us to what God intends." This is an unanswerable argument. What do you say to a crucified man or woman? He is not arguing with you. He is just setting an example. What can you say to his family who is willing to be crucified with him? What can you say to a church willing to be crucified with Christ? They too have stopped arguing with the world.

Rescue and the Church

Rescuers should be recognized by churches in the same way

---

[3] Matthew 16:22-24.

they recognize any other Christian ministry. We should do more than encourage each Christian to personally engage in it to the extent that he has the time and opportunity. Churches should be calling forth people who will devote themselves to protecting children with their lives full time. The elders should examine those who come forward, the way they would examine any missionary. If they find them acceptable as missionaries, they should have a public time of presenting them to the congregation, laying on hands, sending them out, and helping raise the necessary financial support.

We must come to grips with the fact that the iron curtain has fallen on portions of *our* country. It is now illegal to be a public Christian in these sectors. Churches have quietly skirted these zones, or set up alternative structures. Often, Christians explain how godlessness really is the best way in these public areas of life, and that what goes on there is none of our business. One area where the iron curtain has decisively fallen is around the preborn death camps. It is illegal to be a Christian brother to a child whose murder we could easily postpone, or in many cases prevent. This makes it difficult to support missionaries to the people trapped in these dead zones, because society will strike back at any support base for the missionary. We used to get lots of advice from people on how Operation Rescue should be organized and conduct its business. None of it took account of this reality: Rescue makes havoc of incorporation and board structures. Those to whom Rescuers are accountable risk liability for what the Rescuers do. And that is the organizational problem facing all Rescue groups — how do you maintain accountability and support without liability?

But there are ways to minimize the risk of providing support and accountability. For instance, the Rescuer can keep in direct though unofficial touch with you and your elders. You can support him through diaconal funds for the needy. If he is married, you need not give a penny to him; give the diaconal help to his wife for her needy family.[4] The Church *can* act

---

[4] It is still legal to give money to the wife of a Missionary to the Preborn. This may change. For instance, in Russia it used to be illegal even to give food to a minister's family while he was in jail. Fortunately, Russian

wisely with its finances and need not tempt a confrontation with the government. But if it comes to where we must choose to either share liability or stop standing with those who protect children, then you "joyfully accept the confiscation of your property because you yourselves have better and lasting possessions . . . . So do not throw away your confidence . . . ."[5] Having said this, we are a long way from this either/or decision. Supporting a missionary is still a very low-risk ministry.

There is more that the Church can do. Christians can make one phone call a day to the mayor, judge, district attorney, or jailer, and request that these officials stop keeping Christians from protecting children from murder: "Let My people go, that they may serve Me!" As Christian and secular officials meditate on this single message, it may do more to change Church and society than any other single thing we have done.

In the Church or Not at All

As tempting as it is to turn to the model of a crusade outside the Church, it is better to risk the property of the Church than it is to let Rescue become a ministry outside the Church. A crusade will not accomplish what only the Church can do. God longs after His people, His body — the Church. It seemed like a good idea at the time for Sarai to give Hagar to Abram to get the job done and fulfill God's promise. But it was not God's

---

Christians did not base their reasons for feeding their pastor's family on the arguments so many use against Rescue. If they did, they would not have fed their pastor's family.

The argument goes like this: as long as *we* are not *required* to kill the unborn, then their death is only permitted by the state. In other words, if the government does not require *us* to do evil we should not disobey it. With this reasoning, we might argue that, as long as the Communist government — which has the legal responsibility to feed people — does not require the congregation to kill the pastor's family, then they should obey the government and not feed them. As long as the congregation is not *required* to kill their pastors family, then their starvation is only permitted!

For the life of me, I will never understand how it can be so difficult to see that when someone orders you to step back and let a child be murdered — or starved to death — right in front of you, he is ordering you to rebel against God and everything God has made you to be, both as a man in God's image and as a redeemed man in the image of His Son.

[5] Hebrews 10:32-35.

way. The Church is always asking God to be fruitful and fulfill His promises through some hired servant, or relative, whether Hagar or Eliezer,[6] or some crusade, but never through the congregation itself.

One of the common criticisms of Rescue groups was that they seemed to lack organization and planning. This was not due to ineptness on our part entirely. What we preached from 1987 to this day had a consistent emphasis which held us back. We said with the Song of Deborah, "The leaders led in Israel, and the people followed, Praise the Lord!" Our goal was to see churches, not organizations, rise up to defend the children. In the beginning this happened with great success: more pastors were arrested with us than with any other organization in the history of this country. As organizations sprang up, we kept pushing local leaders to put pastors and elders in leadership and minimize the Rescue organization and pray for it to dissolve entirely. The result was organizationally disastrous, but it was the right way to lose.

How can this be? How can we actually prefer to lose with the Church than to win without it? How could anyone truly hoping to win think that the Church would ever overcome its inertia? How could the Church ever deal with child-killing when it stumbles over the basic issues of congregational life? And besides, most churches do not want to be involved. Do we stop everything until they move?

The answer to this is the bottom line of my life. If God does not do it in the Church, He will not do it anywhere. And the Church will only be brought along as far as she sees what we preach matched by what we do.[7]

---

[6] Genesis 15 and 16. This is an ecclesiastical application of Galatians 4:30.

[7] The number of Rescues in a city indicates how prepared the Church is to protect children, whether the Rescuers spend the time between Rescues in jail, or at home. The reason we need people willing to spend months in jail for a single Rescue, is not to clog the courts or jails, but to raise the moral stakes for all of us. In jail he becomes a visible representative of the child in the womb who is still invisible to the Church. The Rescuer in jail is no longer the one standing between the killer and the victim; now some- one must stand in the gap for them, freeing the missionary to rescue again. Moral authority, not clogged courts and jails, will turn the tide. Standing

I do not have any plans for success apart from God's changing hearts of stone to hearts of flesh. It does not matter that it is Christians who need a heart transplant. The most famous evangelistic text, from Revelation 3:20, "Behold I stand at the door and knock," was not written to unbelievers, but to the Church. To protect the preborn from the apathy of the American Church itself, God is prepared to remove our lampstand. The book of Revelation does not present the Church with the option of leaving the door closed, as so many evangelists misapply this verse to their unsaved hearers. No, Jesus Christ is coming through that door whether we open it or not. It is His Church and His door. If we do not open it in a communion of heartfelt obedience, then He will blast it in and remove us, as He would waft away an odious stench from His nostrils — for this is what our prayers will become to Him, filtered through the bloody screams of the little ones as they are ushered into His presence.[8]

I pray that the Church will see, in the visible bonds of the bars and chains of jail which prevent us from protecting children, the far greater invisible bonds of their willful cooperation with abortion binding them from protecting the preborn themselves or protecting them through us. At least let the Church see in us a picture of what is coming to her if she does not stand today for others.

Exorcism: The Prophetic Ministry of the Church

There are three kinds of exorcism in the New Testament. In one, the exorcists fail and are either discouraged, or are thrown from the house naked and bleeding because they have all the best intentions and strategies, but no power. In another, the exorcism is a success, but there is nothing to replace the demon and he returns with seven demons worse than he is. And finally, there is the removal of the foul spirit and its replacement with God's Holy Spirit.[9]

---

on principle, we give the Church an opportunity to move.

[8] Isaiah 1:10-15; Micah 3:1-4; Jeremiah 11:9-16; Amos 5; Rev 2 and 3.

[9] Matthew 17:14-21; 27:55-56; 28:1-10; Mark 16:1-10; Luke 8:2; 9:38-42; 11:24-26; 24:1-10; John 15:25; 20:1-18.

I see the current establishment pro-life groups as being the first sort of exorcism — all the best intentions and sincerity but with solutions which never come close to matching the demonic horror. The second type of exorcism is the popular-crusade approach. It seemed good in the Middle Ages as a way to take the Holy Land for Christ. Crusades certainly streamline your effort and get it away from stodgy church governments. But they do not replace the demon with something lasting. Operation Rescue can easily fit into this pattern. Rescue should put fire back into the cultural imagination of men and inspire them to live by the standards that make civilization possible. But a crusade will only short-circuit this process. The Church must be matured to bear the weight of authority God has prepared for it.

The only solution is what Daniel foresaw: not a crusade, but the expansion of the kingdom of God itself to fill the earth. Those with this vision willingly suffer faithfully for righteousness sake until God ignites this vision again in the heart of His Church . . . or simply obliterates us here in America and starts again, perhaps even in another part of the world. It would not be the first time. The current stage of the evangelization of Africa has made it very similar to 6th Century Europe. Give God 1,000 years, and He might do considerably more with Africa than He did with barbarian Europe in the same amount of time — especially if they learn from our lesson.

Until the Church takes on its historic role, inspiring her sons and daughters to be utterly intolerant of evil, it will never become the civilization-creating force God intended it to be. It will only be a parasite sucking the blood out of those who have gone before. This is why, in weighing what I will do with my life and influence, such as it is, I can see no more effective plan than living as if these words are true. There is not much more to say. But much more to do. As I write this in 1991, I am very skeptical of ever seeing these words published. And if they are published, I am skeptical of their penetrating anyone's heart. That is why I must return to the death camps even of a city like Atlanta; because once there, I am in a place where we can proclaim the loudest that there is no pit so deep that God is not deeper still. The missionaries there bear witness in the name of the Church of Jesus Christ that He will move in His time to revive His people and transform this city, making it safe for children. Until then, we have Jesus' question in Luke 18:8 to meditate on, "When the Son of Man comes, will He find faith on the earth?"

The Cross, the Prophet, and the Church

The question is not, "Are we too radical?" The real question is, "Are we faithful enough?" Read the prophets. They speak graphically of Israel's unfaithfulness to God, in terms of adultery and excrement smeared on the faces of priests.[10] Isaiah preached in the nude for three years. Ezekiel spent a year lying on his side to illustrate the coming siege of Jerusalem. Hosea married a whore. Jesus called the religious leaders of His day — that is, all of us who think we are trying to set an example of Biblical piety — white-washed tombs, blind guides, snakes, vipers, and hypocrites. He walked into the middle of the temple, ran the moneychangers out, *and then He bodily blocked the entrance — refusing to let them carry on their lawful business.*[11]

Imagine Jesus or any of the prophets — real men — complaining that their ministries seemed to be getting nowhere. They all had the talent to make a real success of their ministry. Would we have advised them to read *How to Win Jews and Influence Greeks*? Would we have advised them to change their

---

[10] Ezekiel 23, most of Hosea, and Malachi 2:3 — among other places. To appreciate the unenviable public relations task of the prophets, check *Strong's Concordance* under adultery, whoring, and dung. Now imagine publicly describing any of *your* church's sins in these same terms.

[11] Mark 11:15-19. "Jesus entered the temple area and began driving out those who were buying and selling there . . . *and he would not allow anyone to carry merchandise through the temple courts.*" There is nothing in Moses to indicate that it is unlawful to facilitate temple worship by providing sacrifices for Jews from far countries, and changing their money to enable them to buy those sacrifices. And yet He forcefully stopped what even *God's* law permitted! If the body is the temple of the Holy Spirit; if abortion then is the mass destruction of temples God is preparing for His glory; then perhaps this passage would be normative for how we should act at the desecration of God's little temple in the womb. It certainly shows Jesus blocking the doors, not letting anyone into the temple who would be doing the wrong thing, like carrying burdens through it, or murdering little ones.

church growth strategy? Would we tell Elijah to get elected (or anointed) and work within the political process instead of starving out in the desert, committing gross acts of civil disobedience himself, and then having the effrontery to accuse God's properly anointed king of civil disobedience?[12] Judging from how little the Church wishes to imitate the prophets' ministries today, we can only assume that today's Christian judges those ministries to have been failures. And like their fathers before them, they would throw out any who dared imitate Jesus and the prophets. Yet then or now, God's true prophets never had God's blessing to walk out on His people. They set us the example of staying within the confines of the Church of their day without toning down their message. Anyone who considers himself prophetic must do the same.

Would to God the American Church fails in its ministry the ways these men failed — because she has become too hard-hitting and offends the world with the Cross; not because she whines and begs to be left alone with the freedom to worship and nice buildings to worship in. Would to God those who have a prophetic ministry today overcome their bitter disappointment and not abandon the Church to form their own little schisms. Let us never fail because we had neither the courage to stand up, nor the long-term vision to remain faithfully standing.

Our situation is desperate, requiring not years but generations of sacrificial obedience to dig out of it. Our situation requires nothing less than the conversion of our families, our businesses, and our politics — indeed, the very conversion of the Church itself — to Christianity. Not sit-ins, not activism, not the revival hour, strong preaching and strong singing, but old-fashioned, take-up-your-cross-and-follow-Me Christianity. The pattern of the Cross is the pattern for the Church, therefore we will do what we have to do in the Church or not at all. God will not abandon His bride, nor can we.

---

[12] "Is that you, O troubler of Israel?" said Ahab. To which Elijah replied, "I have not troubled Israel, but you and your father's house have, in that you have forsaken the commandments of the LORD!" I Kings 18:17-18.

SECTION II

ISSUES OF THE CROSS

It is not enough to determine whether or not the *world* permits something. We have to ask whether God allows *us* to permit it.

We tend to approach the question of intolerance backwards. When you are dealing with mass killers and their protectors, you must justify those points at which you tolerate and cooperate with them, not those points at which you do not tolerate them. The day may come when we are in danger of being too intolerant of child-killers. Until then, what must be explained is why we are so cooperative with them.

Chapter 5

ENDING IDOLATRY:
THE PRICE OF THE CROSS

God Jus' Gonna Have to Unnerstan'

Take Slim. He was an engaging young man who could talk his way into or out of most anything. He shared my cell for two months and to hear him you'd think that jail was just a momentary problem. Of course he would never wind up back in here again. In fact, God was going to get him out soon, he was confident, because God is a good and merciful God, and Slim was His son — and a Presbyterian at that.

Slim was not that bad. True, he had sex with an awful lot of women. But they all seemed to love him and understand, and he was very gentle and compassionate with them. He really liked them. Drugs were just fun and harmless enough. He was able to work for a good living. He was proud of his college education and his ability as a bricklayer.

His doctrine was orthodox. He loved the Lord too, with all his heart, and we would often pray and read the Bible together. I thought that surely this good man — like American society — just needed a little more education, and so we would study together. We reviewed over the months what it meant to be a Christian.

Then one day, we were studying I Corinthians 6, "No whore-monger, adulterer, etc. shall inherit the kingdom of heaven." Slim looked at me and said, "Rev, I believe in God jus' the same as you. I know that sex and rocks [crack cocaine] is sin. But I know that God forgives sinners, otherwise I cain't be saved. I confessed my sin, an' I prayed for God to give me a new heart. So I guess God is jus' gonna have to unnerstan' that I need that sh-- to get along, that's all. God jus' gonna have to unnerstan'."

I was stunned at how simply he could put it without blinking an eye. Here was a man who had neatly combined salvation by grace with free sex and drugs. But it was not *his* audacious feat

61

which stunned me. What hit me was the voice of the Church speaking through him.

What Slim meant, of course, was that he could count on Good ol' God to keep on accepting him the way he was, even though he refused to give up what to him were the good things of this world. We are shocked at the presumption of someone who thinks that God will wink at persistent physical fornication and drugs. But are we as shocked at Christians who have drugged their hearts and minds with materialism? Have we ever said, "God just has to understand and accept our spiritual fornication with the good things of life because we cannot give them up to be a light in this world — to protect the unborn, to bring an end to pornography, to transform the entire government and education system — to bear witness sacrificially to the saving grace of Jesus Christ to lost souls?" Do we say, "We've confessed our sin and prayed for God to give us a new heart. So I guess God will jus' have to unnerstan' that we cain't risk all the good things o' this life jus' to obey Him by loving our neighbor as our selfs. We need this [stuff][1] to get along, that's all. God jus' gonna have to unnerstan'." Is that what we say? Am I a bright light for Christ except where it gets threatening to my things, and assume, of course, that good ol' God unnerstans? He was once flesh like us. Right? The kingdom of God is the blessing of meat and drink? Right?

My eye wandered down that passage, "uncleanness, jealousy, wrath, factions" and I thought about other similar verses which include gossip, bearing a grudge, even cowardice, and drawing back, which "God jus' has to unnerstan'" in our lives. Far beyond our failure to be a light to the world, we have built our personal lives on the same arrogant belief that God

---

[1] The delicate Christian is often shocked when God calls the things of this world the same thing Slim calls them — their indelicate, yet quite proper, name. As Philippians 3:8 puts it, "What things were gain for me I count as loss for Christ. Yea doubtless, I count all things but loss for the excellency of the knowledge of Christ Jesus my Lord: for whom *I have suffered the loss of all things, and do count them but dung, that I may win Christ.*" Thus the Apostle on even the good things we might use to justify ourselves for disobeying God. Perhaps if we called all our [stuff] what God and Slim call it, materialism would not be rotting us out so effectively.

cannot take care of us if we actually obey Him — and so we gossip, bear a grudge, or fear to call a judge to account. How deep is our fornication against Him just on the level of our personal sins? How many gods infest our pantheon? How much does our fear to rescue only reveal the fact that we need rescuing from all these other gods first?

Does God overlook and understand Slim's excuses and save him? Does God understand the excuses of the American Church — or my personal excuses in the matter of individual holiness and obedience — and save us? The whole matter of being Rescued from bondage to the other gods in our life — whether the gods of sex and drugs, or the gods we make of our house, job, church building, and the American Way — is bound up in the question of authority.

It does no good to protest that houses and jobs are not sinful in and of themselves as Slim's gods of sex and recreational drugs are. Nothing may excuse us to disobey God, whether it is a good thing in and of itself or a sinful thing in and of itself. Do these other good things become gods to us by taking authority in our lives, permitting us to disobey God? If so, they are idols.

List them separately:

1) Does a government have the God-like authority to command us to protect murderers?

2) Does our house have God's authority to command us to protect abortionists lest we lose it in a lawsuit?

3) Does our church building, or ministry, have God's authority to forgive us for letting children be murdered because our ministries were more important than their lives?[2]

4) Does our family have authority to replace God by threatening to disintegrate if we put God first and lay down our lives to protect His little ones?

5) Are we really putting our families first in a Biblical way when we use them to justify why we must protect the rights of child-killers instead of the rights of the children being killed?

---

[2] "Is this the kind of worship God requires?" asks Isaiah 58:1-14; 1:10-17.

In all of these ways we make idols of our families, laws, houses, and ministries. These idols usurp God's authority, commanding us to preserve them with the blood of children.

If God calls Slim's attempt to maintain his way of life "physical fornication," will He not call our attempt to maintain our way of life "spiritual fornication?" Will He find either acceptable? Can either of us escape judgment?

Who has authority to *refuse* to turn God's blessings into idols? Who may refuse to commit spiritual fornication with them? That depends on who authorizes us to protect the innocent versus who authorizes us to protect their killers.

Who Authorized You *Not* To Rescue?

Clearly the onus is not on the one who saves a life to prove why it is right to do so. The burden is on those who oppose saving a life to show that they are not clinging to idols for their own justification.

To cut to the heart of the matter we may ask, "Why — by what right and in whose name — can we claim authority to stop a child-killer when the *government* has made killing legal and protects these killers with its police, courts, and jails?"

This is a question of *authority*: does God in His Word give you the authority to protect a child's life? If so, is *your* authority to protect the child greater than the *state's* authority to compel you to protect the child's killers?

Some say the state has the authority to stop you at a property line and prevent your going farther to save a baby from being murdered. Not to stop at that line, they say, is rebellion against God, Who has handed to human authorities — the state — the authority to protect child-killing. In other words, if asked by God, "Why didn't you try to physically rescue these children? Why did you join with the state in protecting their killers by stopping your activities at the property line?" they believe they can confidently answer God, "Because You gave us no *authority* to protect these children when the state commands us to protect their killers."

The problem with this understanding of authority is that there are no instances in Scripture where a human government at any level was given the authority[3] to frame laws which protect those who kill its innocent citizens. In fact, the exact opposite of this is the case. Much of Scripture deals with the judgment God brings against the rulers who frame such laws, against the people who obey them, and even against those who tolerate those laws by permitting them to be obeyed by others.

The implication of this is clear. Because God has not given the state the authority to pass laws that defend those who slay the innocent, then when Christians rescue the innocent, they are clearly not in conflict with any authority which God has given the state. *What is more, if the state does not have the authority to command you to disobey God by protecting baby-killers, then it has no authority to justify you when God calls you to account for protecting the killers.* Romans 13 establishes the limit for governing authorities: "Reward good and punish evil." Coercing people to protect child murder is not good unless you make the state your idol. Therefore the state has no *authority* to make it right for you to protect child-killers, even though it might have the *power* to punish you for stopping the killers.

The Challenge: Let the Children Speak for Themselves

Though there are hundreds of reasonable answers to those who claim that Christians have no authority to protect the innocent from murder, I have discovered that most people are neither for nor against Rescue because of the dictates of cold reason. So, we must let the children speak for themselves.

For most people, it is enough to say, "Abortion is murder." The rest follows. But if you believe that abortion is murder, while at the same time believing that we must obey laws which protect each public murder, try this: write to *Human Life International*,[4] ask for one of their postcards of a dead child,

---

[3] Do not confuse authority with power. Governments have the power to do whatever they have the power to do, but this does not mean that God has authorized them, or that He authorizes His people to obey them, at those points where they exceed their authority. Luke 23:28-31, ". . . weep for yourselves and for your children," makes it clear that *all* Jerusalem would be judged, along with those who actually rejected and crucified Him.

[4] Human Life International, 7845-E Airpark Rd, Gaithersburg, MD 20879.

and put it on your bathroom mirror. Forget this or any other book. Let the child speak for himself.

This is perhaps my most offensive challenge. I do not believe that anyone can do this for long and continue to object to Rescue. There may be a thousand reasons why we do not set up that picture, but they all boil down to one: We cannot. We do not have what it takes to listen to the testimony of this child for even five minutes a day and still say it is wrong to physically protect him. I am not making a moral argument here, I am simply stating a fact: you cannot do it without his changing your life. If you think I have wrongfully condemned you of a moral lapse, then you need to examine why you think being unable to look a dead child in the eye is a condemnation.

*What has happened to us? There was a time when the only argument we had about babies was whether or not to baptize them. How is it that now in the Church itself we are seriously arguing that it is wrong for someone to physically protect babies from murder? And why is it that so many leaders feel a need to defend why **they** are not doing it by condemning those who do try to save these children's lives?*

"But who is condemning whom?" asks the nonrescuer. "This whole book is a condemnation of those who don't do sit-ins!"

No. It is a book about *why* people refuse to sit-in at abortion clinics. It is about how sitting-in can reflect a God-centeredness to our lives, which no other activity yet proposed can. *It is also about how sitting-in can be just another idol.* God wants our hearts, not our treasure, not even our sit-ins, because He knows that where our heart is there will our treasure be also. This book is about the Cross in all of our lives — not just in the pro-life part, or the Sunday morning part — manifesting a fearlessness toward those who can destroy only the body, and a reverent fear toward Him who can destroy body and soul. Idolatry — looking to something other than God to save or provide for us — cuts us off from God, not just in the small realm where the idol rules, but finally in our whole life, twisting and stunting it — because neither God, nor His creation, will tolerate a rival authority.

Five American Idols in Our Hearts and Churches

There are five blessings of God which have become idols in the sanctuaries of our churches and lives. The Cross threatens them. We will either put them in their proper place, or God will put us in our proper place of judgment.

Today, there is a growing number of people who no longer assume that being human has any fundamental connection with having a right to life, liberty, or the pursuit of happiness. How can the Church speak to them with integrity if we worship the same gods? *If we purchase our freedom to do what we want to do — worship, build buildings, be incorporated and tax exempt, have ministries, and "obey God" — at the expense of permitting doctors to kill babies, why should not the world purchase its freedom to do what it wants to do by killing babies?* Ask not for whom the mother sacrifices her child. When we dig to the bottom of our idolatry, we find not gross sin, but the good things we have permitted to replace God:

1) *The idolatry of thinking that* **man's** *laws can save us.* From where does the idea come that if we just seize the reins of political power in the land, then we can make it illegal to kill the unborn? When you get to the point of 50 million Christians watching public murder, something is as rotten in their heart as it is in the Supreme Court. A mere change in the court or in its decrees will not deal with the desperate rottenness of our hearts.

Moses might have become the next Pharaoh and brought legal emancipation to Hebrew slaves. But God knew that Pharaoh's law could never free His people from the slavery which dwelt in their heart. He knew that pagan or secular governments could not grant true freedom to His people. When God's people look to the governments of the world for freedom, they become slaves looking to Egypt, Chaldea, or the American Constitution for liberty, rather than to the Word of God. This slavery always asks the laws of the nations to define what is permissible and impermissible for the Christian. It says, "Show us the way, O nations of the earth, that we may walk in it." God knew that only a desert could begin a process of sanctification, still going on today — 4,000 years later. We, His people, still hate that desert as much as ever. We are still sniveling about how God can bless us even if we stay out of the desert. "Egypt isn't that bad," we say. "We still have a lot of freedom here, and the food's great! Besides, God calls some people to stay in Egyptian slavery." Or we bravely go into the desert only to start whining around, looking for some way to get out without having to face the giants in the land. Instead, Moses identified with God's people against the "law" of Pharaoh. He preferred suffering and reproach with God's people to all the treasures of Egypt. He would not tolerate a citizenship on earth which forfeited his citizenship with God and identification with God's people.

Daniel, like Moses, also refused to identify with the world against God. Can you hear the Jewish elders approaching Daniel to remind him that God had given him political obligations which should not be thrown away by breaking a *temporary* injunction against prayer: "But Daniel, it is just thirty days that you cannot pray. If you throw away the political stewardship God has given you, then who will protect Israel from men like Haman? God has put you *here*. God has not given you a lion's-den ministry!"

Can you hear Daniel's scorn: "You blind elders! You think the lions you can see are the ones which can hurt me? They can only crush flesh and bone. It is the political lions you cannot see whom you ought to fear — they consume your very soul for a compromise. You say God has put me here? So He has. And if I am to be faithful to Him politically, if I am to be strong enough to protect your skins from persecution, then I must be strong enough to stand up to mere physical lions, or I will never have what it takes to withstand the test in the political arena where spirit and soul are bought and sold." Daniel knew that politics is not where God's man flees to avoid suffering, persecution, and lions' dens. Politics for the Christian is not where you make "real changes." It is simply where you have to do what is right even though you lose your life . . . or the next election.

How many times have we heard, "The *real* solution to abortion is to change the laws!" This can be idolatry. Are we who are afraid to lay down our lives for our neighbor fit to wield political power? "If we can just seize the power bases," we mutter to ourselves, "we can make everything right." Thus "change the law" becomes little more than a mantra to our new god, "Law-and-Order." Maybe he can make it so that we do not have to take up our cross in this generation. Maybe Law-and-Order can enable us to Rescue our possessions and save babies too.

It will be deadly for us if we grasp after earthly power — whether through normal politics within the system, or sit-ins outside the system — without stopping to earn the godly character needed to wield such power wisely. The world tantalizes us with the hope of ruling its kingdoms, if we would only rule Satan's way, and worship him. God's offer to us is seldom as pleasant or hopeful: it is a cross and a kingdom, founded in heartfelt loving obedience at any cost. Only out of the standards of the righteousness and sacrifice of His Cross can politics become Christian, redemptive, and fruitful. All too easily the world proves that we are not willing to lay down our lives for others, only our laws. If they can prove this, then they are correct to suspect that our political solutions will be little more than the forcing of others, through law, to carry burdens we will not lift even a little finger to carry ourselves: We ask the young mother to sacrifice for us either her child through abortion, or her way of life by bearing the unwanted child.

The solution to legalized murder must go deeper than a mere law against it. This is how politics can become a false god, a false solution to abortion (or any other social evil), whitewash on a tomb. Yes, we must change the law, *but never as an excuse to avoid taking up the Cross*. In fact, only Cross-bearers in the political arena — those who do not worship man's laws, law courts, or voters' whims — will be able to change it.

2) *The idolatry of thinking that saying the right words or pushing the right education program can save us*. We must do more than make people aware that the unborn are human. We must raise up a generation which will do what it takes personally and corporately to defend the innocent. Our society's legal and social structure is built on the foundation of the sanctity of all human life and the personal responsibility of each citizen to protect his neighbor. This foundation stone — that all men are created equal and are obligated to protect one another — was not the insight of secular men, but is itself rooted in the more pro-found cornerstone on which Christ built His Church.

In Matthew 16, Jesus said that Peter's confession, "You are the Christ, the Son of the living God," would serve as the cornerstone of the Church and nothing could prevail against it. Peter did not realize that intrinsic to being the Messiah-King was the requirement that He lay down His life for His people. So in the next breath, Jesus had to rebuke Peter for wanting to build the Church on a different cornerstone. Jesus played on the idea of two stones by calling Peter's rejection of the Cross a "stumbling stone" and called Peter "Satan" for even suggesting it. The Cross — dying to ourselves and living for our Lord, laying down our lives for each other — this is the foundation of the Church. Against these things the gates of hell will not prevail. The Captain of our salvation leads in these matters — He is the Cornerstone. We align our lives on Him as stones are aligned on the cornerstone. The Biblical basis of equality is that we serve one another. Jesus ended His comments to Peter that day by saying, "If *any* man would be My disciple, let him take up his cross and follow Me."

If words could make us free, then men would not have died because of the Gospel, or for the Declaration of Independence, or anything else. At best, words can only survey the path of freedom. They cannot walk it for you. If a constitution could make men free, then the 75 banana republics which have constitutions much like ours would be free. If education could make us free, then Jesus would not have bothered to die; He would simply have set up a new and better rabbinical school.

The religious root of the Declaration of Independence is its fundamental principle of law, making our civilization possible — the universal call to lay down our lives for the least of these among us. This is what equality means. We must live as if we are equal neither by *chance nor choice*. It is because God *created* us equal that we have rights. We have inalienable rights only because we are endowed with them by our *Creator*. It is because He took up His Cross for us that there is any chance of these concepts leavening the society. Only when the Church lives or dies as if this is true, does the world have any hope of experiencing political freedom.

This religious cornerstone, and the political house built on it, are under serious attack in this nation because we have reduced ourselves to mere words. Those who kill people who are useless to them are no longer afraid to use *our* terms and admit that those they kill are "human." Our abortion/euthanasia culture is no longer afraid of the implications of destroying unwanted human life. They are unafraid of any who might oppose them with cheap words. For the humanist, the value of preborn human life is negligible compared to the value of the life-*style* of the mother. Though the American Church may want to answer the world in the name of the Living God, our words fall to the ground: we affirm the humanity and equality of the preborn, yet refuse to protect them. For the Church today, the value of a child's life is negligible compared to the value of the life-*style* of the Christian. Other things are more important than the children's lives. Things — like the world's respect, tax exemption, not getting sued, and our "ministry" — these things are more valuable to us than the very life of our unborn neighbor.

And this is why the solution to legalized murder must go deeper than mere words and pictures which educate people. Our words alone will never build liberty and justice for all. Education cannot justify our failure to lay our lives down. Education that does not lead to lives laid down is a false god, a false solution to abortion or to any other evil.

3) *The idolatry of thinking that "stewardship" in the Church can save us by excusing our disobedience.* Most of the Church's "good reasons" for not protecting children come under the category of being a good steward of our buildings, budgets, ministries, programs, and people. We have put stewardship of our ministry-related possessions and careers above human life. Can you imagine Jesus telling the Pharisees in Mark 2:27:[5] "God did not create possessions to serve man; He created man to serve his possessions!"? Apparently the Church today can. As we echo the Pharisees of Mark 7:6-13, we self-righteously declare, "Corban!" to the preborn. And so we set aside God's law for our traditions: "What we would have to lose to protect you, we preserve so that we can live comfortably in large

---

[5] "The Sabbath was made for man, not man for the Sabbath."

Churches and devote ourselves to our great Gospel ministry which God has blessed." Do I say this because possessions are wrong or the Gospel should not be preached? Of course not. The Pharisees were not wrong for wanting to hallow the Sabbath or support the temple. They were wrong for thinking God is hallowed by ministry, worship, buildings, and budgets established at the expense of innocent human life where these victims could have been rescued. The work of the kingdom must not be used as an excuse to let someone kill a baby in public.

The solution to legalized murder must go deeper than plans which do not threaten our ministries, buildings, and programs. Otherwise, stewardship becomes a false god, a false excuse to permit abortion or any other social evil — a false way to keep our spiritual possessions and ministries. In the name of being a good steward in the kingdom, we justify our making idols of them, and finally making love to them.

4) *The idolatry of thinking that activism — **doing the right things** — will save us.*   Rescue does not make us right with God. The act of sitting-in itself must not be treated as the act to absolve us of blood-guiltiness. If we preach Rescue at the abortion clinic as if it were the totality of righteousness, then we who Rescue there have been found with another form of idolatry — the whole body being reduced to one part. We must always keep the prophetic edge of our ministry sharp and not become recruiters for some new activist strategy. Activism cannot become God. Where Rescue is reduced to an activist strategy, at best it loses its prophetic edge; at worst, it becomes an idol.

Ultimately, laying down your life for another is not a strategy. It is God's design for His kingdom. Dying to self is not a matter of the special calling of the activist. It is the pattern for Christian living. "Dying to self" must not become the exclusive code word for "anti-abortion sit-in." If, as different parts of the body of Christ, we were truly, faithfully dead to ourselves in each area where God has called us, then mere jail, fines, or the seizing of our houses would have been irrelevant to our willingness to Rescue the preborn — accepting loss for God's sake would be a way of life. Yes, dying to self has strategic implications, but we lose the power of any strategy derived from it if we reduce it to an activist strategy. The irreducible core is that we must protect the innocent in theory and in real life, in legal institutions and in history, in Sunday school and in the street.

The solution to legalized murder must go deeper than activism and sit-ins. Otherwise, these activities can become a false god, a false solution to abortion or any other social evil.

5) *The idolatry of thinking that preserving God's material blessings in our personal life is a reason God will accept for our permitting murder.* Do we accuse the abortionists of worshipping the god of Money? Then we accuse ourselves, to the extent that we draw back from protecting children for fear of losing the favor of the Money god if we get fined or sued. Do we accuse the women who seek abortions of sacrificing their infants to the gods of Career, Family Name, Respectability, Nice Things, or Mere Convenience? Then we only accuse ourselves when we refuse to risk our careers, family peace, respectability, nice things, and convenience to save these children. Far be it from us to incur the wrath of our local 20th Century deities — Baal Money, Baal Status, Baal Family Time.

Do the abortionists and the women seeking to murder their children worship the God of the State by letting what is merely legal dictate their moral choices? Then our obeying trespass laws and injunctions becomes that much more an act of homage to our new lord, Baal State, by letting his protection of child murder dictate our moral response as we join in the protection scam. To the extent that we draw back to protect any part of our life-style instead of protecting the children, we purchase that part of our life by infant sacrifice. The mortar we use to hold the bricks of our life together is mixed with the blood of the children. The mother's sacrifice of her child, which we might have prevented but did not, becomes our sacrifice with her to our mutual gods.

This will seem harsh and judgmental only if we do not take into account that the same God who commanded these women and their doctors saying, "Thou shalt not kill!" has commanded us to be our brother's keeper, to love our neighbor as ourselves, to defend the fatherless, to rescue the innocent, to do unto others as we would have them do unto us; in a word, to have the mind of Christ.[6] All the reasons for not protecting children may be, in and of themselves, the good blessings God promised us — money, possessions, a good reputation, social stability, honoring the governor, a good job, an active ministry. They are all good, until they are bought with something other than the blood of Christ, and grasped after, as if they could cleanse us of our sin of blood-guiltiness on that day when we must give an account of why we rescued our blessings, instead of the innocent.

The solution to legalized murder must go deeper than limiting our efforts to those actions which do not threaten God's blessings to us. Otherwise, these blessings — given by God's hand — become false gods, false authorities which cannot justify us. They give a false confidence that God will not spew us and our "blessings" from His mouth as we spewed His little ones from our lives.

Who will justify us on that day when He says, "Why should I not judge you according to your own measure? Insofar as you did not find My brethren worth suffering to protect in this life, I do not find you worth suffering to protect in the next." What god will we then call to be our defense attorney? the Money god? the Reputation and Career god? the Stewardship god? the Political god? the Education god? the Ministry God? the Law-and-Order god? the Convenience god? Where are our building programs now? Where is our reputation? our money? our Ph.D.s, our Th.D.s, our D.D.s? our pastors, elders and governors who convinced us that we had better things to do than worry about abortion? Of these things we made our mighty fortress in this life — a fortress which systematically excluded His little ones — let them protect us. Whose blood will cover our sin? The blood of Him who said, "Inasmuch as you did not do it unto one of the least of these My brethren,[7] you did not do

---

[6] Deuteronomy 5:17; Matthew 5:21-22; Genesis 4:2-12; Luke 10:27-28; I John 3:10; Proverbs 31:8-9; 24:10-12; Psalm 82; Isaiah 1:15-17; Philippians 2.

[7] When a child is aborted, he will go to one of two places. **If** you believe that a pre-born child is unsaved, **then** you think he goes to hell. If what you say is true, you are obligated to rescue him in order give him the possibility of hearing the Gospel — he will see it acted out in the Rescue itself. It is appropriate that we send missionaries to them, reaching

it unto Me. Depart from Me, you cursed, into everlasting fire prepared for the devil and his angels"?[8]

Idols never look like idols to those who depend on them in hope of surviving the problems and realities of everyday life. All five of these idols in the Church are actually God's blessings to which we have bowed down — an excellent political system,

---

through the iron curtain of American law the same way we send missionaries to other places where it is illegal to be a Christian, and thereby reach those for whom it is illegal to hear the Gospel or see the manifestation of its power in someone's life. Matthew 28:20 compels us to rescue him. But on the other hand, **if** you say that the aborted children are bound for heaven, **then** *our* ability to abandon them suggests that *we* rather than *they* are in danger of damnation. For if they go to heaven, they are the brethren of our Lord. Matthew 25:45 says that to abandon them is the same as abandoning our Lord — and verse 46 says that those who abandon their Lord have no reason to be secure in their own salvation.

My purpose here is not to argue the question of the eternal destination of murdered babies, but rather to press you to consider the implications of *your* theology for what *you* will do about the danger their souls are in if *you* believe they go to hell, and what *you* will do about the danger *your* soul is in if you believe they go to heaven.

[8] Matthew 25:31ff does not teach salvation by works, and neither do my comments suggest it here or anywhere else. The only salvation Jesus offered is one which changes lives. The saved person will not — cannot — harden his new heart to those in need of his protection and ministry when they are so close at hand, and their danger so vividly clear. He cannot and will not chose his own safety, well-being, or comfort over theirs. The saved person is a son, not a hireling. *Therefore, an acid test of whether or not we have actually accepted Jesus when we claim to have been born again is whether or not we accept or reject those with whom He identifies — His brethren.* Conversely, *because* we accept Jesus, we minister protection to His brethren. Those who go to the outer darkness are lost, not because they failed to do a good deed, but because their hearts were left stony and unredeemed regardless of how they made a pretense of their salvation. Like the goats, they persistently refuse to see Jesus where He said His presence was obvious. This can only mean that because they never knew Him, they could never recognize Him, and correspondingly, He does not know them nor recognize them on judgment day. This passage is spoken to those in *the visible Church* who had grounds to be satisfied that they were truly members of His covenant family — true believers. They would defend themselves by crying, "Lord, Lord! Did we not do great works and prophesy in Your Name?" These words come to us who would comfort ourselves with the idea, "At least the aborted children go to Heaven." These words may some day rise up before the judgment seat to condemn us as our Lord asks: "You knew that they were My brethren? You knew that I would separate sheep from goats based on what you did to one of the least of these My brethren? And you comforted yourself with this testimony of your own damnation?"

outstanding educational opportunity, good stewardship of the
Church's wealth and ministry, freedom for a wide range of
activism, and personal material blessing undreamt of in the
history of the world. But they will never feed or justify us in
this life or the next. Pointing out these same idols in Israel got
the prophets killed, because God's people would not permit those
prophets to touch what had become holy to them. Idolatry is
"looking for ultimate justification, sanctification, wisdom,
blessing, and authority — in this life or the next — from anything other than God."

Whose covenant will sustain us: our covenant with God, or
our covenant with the gods of this world?[9] Who alone can
provide for us in all things — the LORD, or the ABORTIONIST
whom I agree to protect? the LORD, or my JOB whom I serve?
the LORD or the HOUSE I build. the LORD, or the FAMILY I
nurture? the LORD, or the CITY I vainly watch? These are the
issues of Christianity and civilization. These are the issues of
Rescue.

---

[9] Hosea 4:6, "*Because* you have forgotten the law of your God, I have
forgotten your children." Hosea 5:11, "Ephraim is oppressed and broken
in judgment *because he willingly walked by human precept.*" Hosea 7:3,
"They make a king glad with their wickedness, and princes with their
lies." Hosea 8:1-4, "He shall come like an eagle against the House of the
LORD, because they have transgressed My covenant and rebelled against
My law. . . . They set up kings, but not by Me; they made princes, but
I did not acknowledge them." Micah 6:16, "For the statutes of Omri are
kept . . . that I may make you a desolation, and your inhabitants a
hissing." These passages tell us that Christians obeying the law of the land
can be God's way of preparing their children and churches for destruction,
along with that land. Remember them the next time you hear someone
confidently tell you that Romans 13 is "God's license to His Church to
protect child murderers who are protected by the state. It could simply be
God letting us become ripe for judgment by allowing us to put our
confidence in Omri's baby-killing statutes, thinking that good ol' God will
bless us anyway — after all, it's not important which law we follow, just
so we follow some official law . . . right? Isaiah 6:9-12.

Chapter 6

MARTYRDOM:

THE WITNESS OF THE CROSS

Building up the Monuments to the Prophets

"NO! CHRISTIANS WILL NOT TRADE THEIR SOULS TO AVOID BEATINGS BY POLICE, THEIR HOUSES BEING SEIZED BY JUDGES, OR SITTING IN JAIL FOR MONTHS OR YEARS. GOD'S CHURCH IS BIGGER THAN ANY THREAT THE WORLD CAN BRING. THERE IS NO PIT SO DEEP THAT GOD IS NOT DEEPER STILL. LET OUR POSSESSIONS AND OUR SKINS BURN! WE WILL NOT SELL OUT OUR LORD."

A speech like this is heroic so long as it comes from days which have safely passed us by. But can't you just hear God's children crying out in agonized faith, like Dietrich Bonhoeffer, like an abolitionist, or like a Christian listening to the roar of the bloodthirsty Roman crowd as he awaits his turn in the arena? Can't you hear them crying out to God in some forgotten jail cell when their friends come to talk them into a more sensible course of action which will preserve the good things of their life? And it makes you feel all brave and goose-bumpily because you are a part of this great Church — willing to die rather than deny her Lord.

And see what such faith has produced: The blessings of God! The greatest missionary country in the world with the wealth and technology to support massive outreach. "Yes, God heard those cries. And," we say to ourselves, "to be honest, we'd risk it all again — I'm sure — if there ever were a *real* need."

It was, no doubt, with similar honest conviction that the Pharisees brought their flowers to the monuments they had built to the prophets: "Great men! Great men!" they muttered. "Now, had *we* been there, we would have backed that Jeremiah right up! We'd have walked with him step for step! . . . Great men!" they muttered as they gathered round the tombs.

77

Like the Pharisees, we bear witness against ourselves as sons of those who murdered the prophets: "Great men, those martyrs. Now if *I* were in ancient Rome," we imagine to ourselves, "I'd have been right there telling Caesar that God, not man, is Lord."

We Have Met the Pharisees, and They Is Us

This is why I have a difficult time condemning the police officers who beat us, or the judges who imprison us, or child-killers who cover us up with lawsuits. I know that they are wrong for doing these things to us, because it is the children who suffer ultimately. But how can I condemn others when I see their sin writ large in my own overwhelming temptation to shrink back?

When I stop to ask, "Whom are these judges and police the agents of: the terrible abortion industry? the secular humanist plot?" I realize, "No. They are agents of you and me, of Pastor Smith and Dr. Jones, Th.D. They are agents of all of us who know better, but nevertheless tolerate murder." It would be one thing if we could just condemn them as pagans, but God gives us no such opportunity for pride. The police, judge, and jailer work for us, yet do we stop them from intimidating Rescuers? But worse still, many in the forefront of crushing Christian Rescuers, are not just Christians, but notable Christians.

Major Burnette, of the Atlanta Police Department for 25 years, kept an open Bible on his desk and certificates of distinguished standing with Bill Gothard on his wall. Assistant Chief of Police Bob Vernon of the Los Angeles Police Department has written books on what it means to be a Christian police officer. Yet, they both personally presided over the systematic torture of thousands of "fellow" Christians. Without discrimination, they ordered that 65-year-old grandmothers, physically handicapped people in wheel chairs, and pregnant mothers, be beaten. Why this urgent need for force? So that women six months pregnant could kill their children without delay. All this was done explicitly in the name of the Lord with the public approval of their pastors.[1] Christians, like prosecutor Lee O'Brien of Atlanta and the prosecutor of Santa Clara County, California, defend abortion from the Scriptures in court "because it's my job." Christian men — like Judge Guarino of Philadelphia, Judge Caskey of Redding, California, or Federal Judge Kelly of Wichita — take their Christian faith seriously and yet do all they can to protect the murder of children in their own communities, giving maximum sentences to rescuing Christians.

I *would* say that the horror of these men is that they are the professional representatives of the church in the legal system of America today. I *would* say that the horror is that they are actively supported and defended by their pastors — some of them quite well known, such as John McArthur or Charles Stanley. This is true and horrible, but it is a bit self-righteous of us to point it out, given our own failure of nerve.

No, the real horror is that those of us who are not legal professionals are just as bought out, just as weighed down by the pressing needs of day-to-day life as are our legal representatives. We cannot live lives that reflect our faith any more than they can. Even though we are not police officers or judges, we come to the same terrible precipice of decision — the children or your job, choose! Most of us are merely simple business men and women, pastors, farmers, contractors, programmers, secretaries, clerks, teachers, home-makers, salesmen of insurance, cars, real estate — the gospel of the good life in its infinite forms. Like our legal representatives, we cannot afford to risk leaving all this good life by risking jail, lawsuits, and beatings . . . we just won't.

We have become the horror: knowing, as few others do, the ghastly slaughter taking place at the heart of motherhood and humanity in each abortion, we *knowingly* close perhaps the

---

[1] In the case of Major Burnette and Assistant Chief Bob Vernon, they have both stated publicly that they were personally confirmed by the leading ministers of our day to whom they looked for guidance — Charles Stanley of Atlanta and John McArthur of Los Angeles. To give Dr. Stanley his due, though he has publicly disagreed with Rescue and has approved of arresting Christians who attempt to save life, he has also denounced police brutality. John McArthur, by contrast, continues to support the brutal measures of Assistant Chief Bob Vernon.

clearest window God has begun to open into the womb — the window of our willingness to share a small, tiny fragment of the suffering of the unborn. Thus we join hands with the Christian judges and officers who see to it that the doors of America's Dachaus stay forced open. We voluntarily draw back, not only from Rescue, but from standing with Rescuers who are brutalized by beatings, jail, and lawsuits. Because we are not there for them, they are not freed to rescue again, and others fear to step up to replace them.

The Window on the Womb

This is what abortion brutality means to me. It is not a very flattering perspective. "If wombs had windows," we pro-lifers say smugly, "there would be no abortion!" Well, wombs do have windows — you. How does your life expose the horror of dismembered children? How does your brokenness reflect their brokenness? How does your unity with them rebuild the ties of a common humanity, which are being sundered in our generation child by child, church by church, school by school, Christian by Christian? What do people see in the window of your life? Do they see the reality of the shattered child? Or do they see the sleek, easy health and comfort of the abortionist snug in the bosom of our society's esteem?

How can I look down on judges and policemen who refuse to use their authority to give these children a hearing in their courts or a chance in the street? How can I condemn, when I put the cares of my world as much above the sacrifice of protecting children as the judges and policemen do?

What is brutality? Brutality is often what God permits to prove the authenticity of His Word and ours. It becomes our crucible. No crucible, no gold. As we walk with the Lord at an abortion clinic, we must not shrink back from treating the brutality to the unborn child as He would. Nor should we be surprised when a measure of the brutality directed against the child becomes directed at us in the form of beatings, injustice in court, and long prison sentences. We should consider these things normal when we chose to "be mistreated along with the people of God rather than enjoy the pleasures of sin for a short time, and regard the disgrace for the sake of Christ as of greater value than the treasures of Egypt."[2]

When injustice threatens us personally, it is tempting to shift attention from the suffering of the unborn to the "suffering" of the Christians who defend them. God preserve us from such "compassion" which turns our focus from their murder to our discomfort, from loss of their life to loss of our privilege.

To put our suffering above the children's, is like confusing a window with the things you see through it. God has made you a window for others to see through your life to the reality beyond. You do not take a window and mount it on a museum wall and autograph it. Our suffering is not an end in itself; it is a window through which we can see clearly what is beyond. By trying to save a life, we become first like a window through which an otherwise indifferent world might see, and then like a portal through which they might enter into a new way of life. We do not want others to admire the door, but to pass through it and become a part of the solution — transformed into the image of God; and, with Him, taking up His Cross and following.

It is not the door or window itself, but the reality beyond that we seek to frame by our lives. Your compassion for the prisoner of Christ in jail must be compassion which reaches through the brutality against that Christian, to do something to prevent the brutal murder of the child, even if that is merely to free that Christian to rescue again.

We should defend fellow Christians from police and court brutality, not to create a climate where we escape persecution, but rather to encourage Christians to be free to obey regardless of the persecution. Our freedom in this or any country does not depend on what the law says. We are as free to obey God in America as in North Korea. The only difference is the nature of the punishment we will receive if we act on our freedom. To

---

[2] Hebrews 11:24-26. Moses — like us — was not engaged in unusual debauchery. His sin in Egypt was to be identified as an Egyptian. He had a privileged status, and for him to cling to it at the expense of standing with the Hebrews was called "enjoying the pleasures of sin." Even though he might be doing all he could to liberate the Hebrews legally, he had to choose between identifying himself with God's people and suffering, or identifying with Egypt and living in relative comfort.

treat the laws of a country as if they give or deny freedom is idolatry. Man's laws can merely reward or punish our freedom in Christ. They never grant, establish, or remove freedom from us. We must either exercise our God-given freedom to protect the innocent, or else *we* are in bondage.

L.A.P.D. Assistant Chief Bob Vernon said to me, "When I put on my blues, I become the property of the state."[3] For him, the law of man takes final precedence over his life. Does this mean that if he dies in his blues the state will justify him before God? Did Los Angeles die to make him a new creature? How free in Christ is he if his commitment to the state prevents him from using his position to obey God — to save a life? But before you condemn him, remember this: he is merely putting into words the way most of us act. When he puts on his blues and gives us an order, most of us act as if we too, along with him, have become the property of the state.

The Martyr's Crown

This is why the martyr lies at the heart of Christian witness. He has remained free in his obedience to God — he witnesses to the finality of Christ's Lordship — regardless of the cost. *If you think there are no pro-life martyrs, it is only because the windows of our lives have been so clouded by activism, and by politics, and sermons, and articles, and books, that we cannot see the true martyrs, the 30 million children slain — much less join their witness.* These children are martyred by us Christians who cling to the American Way at any cost.

God sends each child into the life of his parents to call them away from the deceit of materialism, or the hopeless addiction to raising drug money, or the lure of "free" pleasure, or the lie of meaningful relationships outside of the lifelong commitment of marriage. Each child calls his parents to live in accountability to the living God, to repent and be born again, just as he will be born. The child also subpoenas each of us to testify — "Do you

---

[3] He made this comment in the discussions I held with the police department before Operation Rescue's 1989 Holy Week Rescues in Los Angeles. Judge Caskey of Redding, California, made similar comments about his role as a judge when he sentenced two Christians to two years.

stand with me as my fellow witness, or do you stand with the world?"

Each child is a unique witness to the creative love and care of his Father in Heaven. Each one snuffed out in the womb is struck down for the testimony he brings to his parents . . . and to us. In their death, the children become windows into the murderous selfishness of their parents, the doctors, the police, the courts, and if truth be told, of our own murdering hearts. Every reason a mother uses to justify her act, and the police and judges use to justify their defense of her act, all of us use to justify our protection of their bloody work.

Someone standing in solidarity with the children shatters all our self-righteous dreams. Nobody wants to see a living example proving it possible to be compassionate at any cost. We prefer to believe that in the "real world" there is no other choice for us but to permit public murder. Therefore like the world, Christians often will not tolerate those who refuse to stand by. By not walking away, by being beaten by police, by going to jail, we pay the price of refusing to assist those who seek to silence their still small voices. When we rescue, we join the children in their word of hope to their mothers, fathers, and even to the whole world. As the police beat us, we buy precious time for their mothers, as well as the world, to hear their tiny testimony and turn. As we prefer jail to paying money for our release, we join them in their inability to buy, not their freedom, but their very lives. The Christian's willingness to spend years behind bars opens up a window onto their plight and our coming judgment: "You have more than theoretical value, your life is worth at least three days, three months, or even three years of my life in jail. Because *you* cannot walk away, *I* will not walk away. *I* will not pay bail or fine to be free, because *you* cannot purchase your life, much less your freedom. Because *you* have had *your* rights stripped from you without mercy, *I* will renounce *my* rights in this society and not use my time in court to plead for mercy for *me*, but I will insist on pleading for mercy for *you*." Those years in jail become a picture of what is in store for all of us if we harden our hearts to their cry.

As we see the Christian sitting in jail, his body broken by the brutality of the Christian police officers who were directed by Christian judges, ignored by Christian pastors, and abandoned by fellow Christian laymen, may we all see the far greater injustice in the womb — the wrath of being discovered poured out on the little ones. Such a Christian, simply by imitating Christ, forces us to know beyond doubt that there *is* something *any* of us can do. We can love — and make it possible for others to love more effectively — the child in the womb the way Christ loved us.

As Christians sit in cells bound by the visible walls of concrete and steel, may we see through them the far greater threat to our freedom posed by the invisible walls of our voluntary cooperation with the abortion culture. These invisible walls hold us back from the simple call of the Cross to love our neighbors as ourselves, to do unto them as we would have them do unto us. Our invisible bonds of that cooperation with the child-murdering culture hold us back as surely as the visible walls hold back the missionary who has become a prisoner of Christ.

Who Is Sufficient for These Things?

But let's be practical. How many of us can afford to leave everything and stand with the Church at the door of the death camp? How many of us can afford to lose our jobs, our houses, our church buildings? Isn't it much better just to stand symbolically somehow? This is the example judges like Caskey, prosecutors like Lee O'Brien, and police officers like Bob Vernon have set for us. Furthermore, there is no pro-life or Rescue leader (or follower) who has been truly consistent in standing with the children at all cost. Has anyone set an example we can walk in? Is it even possible?

Yes, it is possible. We have the example of Jesus Christ, and we must continue to strive to walk in it. Regardless of how many times we compromise, we must never accept our compromise as a way of life.

My eight year old son, Joshua, taught me this at the second annual YOuth for America Rescue in Atlanta in the Summer of

1991.[4] Two Rescues were planned for this event. On Friday was a "low risk" Rescue in Chamblee, right outside of Atlanta, where you never get held in jail; to be followed by a "high risk" Rescue on Saturday in Atlanta proper. Chamblee bared its fangs and everyone over seventeen was held in jail. This left about a dozen minors still willing to Rescue on Saturday. They were led by my twelve year old daughter Laurel, and by Steve Rella, a fifteen year old Missionary to the Preborn from Milwaukee.

Rather than quitting (which was my secret hope), they decided not only to Rescue, but to go for the biggest death camp in Atlanta — Midtown Hospital, a four story 60,000 square-foot, seventeen-door facility devoted wholly to killing babies. As Laurel said, "We may as well go to Midtown. With only twelve kids and eight of them under ten we couldn't even shut down the smallest abortion mill. If God wants to stop abortion through us, He may as well do it in the biggest one as the littlest."

At 6:30 the next morning, a few kids took the main entrance, and the rest swarmed the parking lot, talking to the incoming mothers. Soon the death camp staff were leading mothers from door to door and the children were sprinting to get to the door first. The police came and watched from the sidelines in amazement, but did not arrest. I personally saw grown men unlock doors, and then be unable to open them with only one or two kids sitting in front of them. Laurel shouted out, "Did you see that, Dad? I prayed for God to make us heavy as boulders, and He did! He did!"

Around 8:00 a.m. the inevitable began to happen. A hefty contingent of death-scorts had gathered — death advocates who assist mothers in getting their unsuspecting babies past the Rescuers. Mothers began to slip in. The little band of children

---

[4] Abortion has been legal in three states since 1967. Any child born since that time is alive by his mother's choice, not America's. Since 1973 almost every mother is carefully asked by her doctor what she thinks about being pregnant. Translation: *"Would you want us to kill your child or find someone who would kill him for you?"* Even many Christian doctors will discover this information, lest they be sued for a wrongful birth. If you were conceived after 1967 and are alive today, you are a holocaust survivor. **One in three of your neighbors did not survive.**

was overwhelmed.

Along about this time, little Joshua was left all alone to hold a main door while the rest ran to block another entrance before mothers could get to it. Soon, he was surrounded by eight or nine obscene, foul-mouthed death-scorts who began to mock him saying, "Go home, little kid. Your mother's calling you. You should have been aborted. You're not going to save any babies today. You're wasting your time here." One woman kept mumbling a stream of obscenities with no apparent rhyme or reason, each word tumbling out after the other, as if she were compiling an illiterate list of all the filth she knew, giving these kids a summary of her public education.

Then, when a mother came to his door, there was Josh, alone, all forty-five pounds of him fending off a dozen adults. They roughly threw the door open and skinned his hand against the brick wall. The death-scorts laughed and taunted him, "What's wrong? Baby gonna cry? Huh? Awwwww, go home, baby. You can't save babies here anyway, you're a shrimp."

Joshua was crushed. He had completely failed. He always imagined himself to be a brave defender of the weak and helpless, and here, he couldn't even keep a door shut and save a baby. He came face to face with the fact that he was nothing like what he had hoped he would be.

Tears streaming down his face, he walked out of the jeering crowd and up the driveway. I knelt down to hug him as he buried his face against my shoulder, crushed, unequal to the task. We sat down on the curb, crying, with our backs to the death camp. Here we were in Atlanta, full of tens of thousands of big people who could end killing today, and the only ones with the courage to act were these puny little kids.

I was a big person, but I was only a spectator too, just like the rest of them — watching in guilty silence afraid to cross over the line. Oh, I had my good reasons for standing by — we all do. And until Joshua walked out to me I had told myself that it was right for me to stand by and let them die today, because soon I would be rescuing in Atlanta and it would be months before I would see Joshua again on the other side of jail. But that day, Joshua's father was no different from the rest of

Christian America. Thanks to Joshua, I saw myself for what I was, even as he saw himself. We wept for our smallness.

Then practical Laurel walked up. "Dad?" she said, "All the appointments have arrived, three babies have been saved and the rest are in. I don't think there's any reason to stay here and get arrested. Is there another abortion mill we can go to?"

"Yes, there is, if it's before 9:00," I said, looking at my watch. It was 8:30, so I went on to brief the general: "Appointments begin to arrive at 9:00. It's on the second floor of a four story building. There's a single door at the end of the hall on the left-hand side as you get off the elevator. We're going to have to stand out on the street a hundred yards from where they will be putting you into the paddy wagon, but we'll be praying."

"Let's go for it," she said, after consulting with Steve.

I could go on to tell you about how, after they arrived at the second death camp and filled the hall, the arresting officer challenged the children to name one law which made what they were doing right. "If you can, I won't arrest you," he promised.

"God's law." They responded without hesitation, quoting Proverbs, the Golden Rule, and the law of love.

Then speaking for much of the American Church, he told them, "Well, then I got to arrest you. God's law doesn't apply to what you're doing, because God's not here now."

But that isn't why I'm telling you this story. I could also tell you how this same officer was asked by Laurel if he would try to save a drowning child on private property that was posted "NO TRESPASSING." He scratched his head and said, "Well, *maybe* I would."

And all the kids said, "*Maybe? Maybe you'd save a life!?* And you call yourself a police officer?"

But the point of this story is not about how an honest policeman became the spokesman for the Church. It is to tell you what Joshua did with the second chance God gave him, and how he can become an example for all of us.

You or I assessing the odds might have simply gone home in despair. "Rescue doesn't work. It isn't worth the effort. I'm too small. God has a better way. These guys must be crazy.

I've tried it, so I know what I'm talking about." We would rehearse to ourselves the euphemisms of self pity.[5]

"That's right." We would hear the world and the American Church murmur soothingly back to us, "There's no shame. You did your best. You need a sabbatical. Time to go home and tend your own garden. God has called you to lots of other important things. It's not like you're giving up or anything. You did great! A lot more than most would have done!"

But not Josh. The mothers began to pile up outside. The police were going in and out. And then the youngest began to file out of the building, each led by an officer. After seven came out, the next was Josh, dead limp in the arms of a sergeant. He couldn't do much that day, but all 45 scrawny pounds was doing all it could while everyone else walked. Given another chance, Josh was going to be sure that the police would know that the blood spilled that day was fully on their own hands — Joshua was the only one under ten who went limp.

To me, that is what Christianity does in a person — even in a child — it plants hope. Not that we are perfect each time out; not that we never fail; but that we never baptize half-way measures even when they are the best we can do. We always come back. We know that some day, we shall be like Him. Therefore, we always try again until we have done all we can. When our best is not good enough — and it often isn't — we are never released from the responsibility to try again. We can never comfort ourselves with how we did our best. Until the job

---

[5] They are euphemisms because if we just said outright what our words conveyed, their weight would be too heavy to bear. They would make us weep with Joshua who was too young to think in euphemisms and so bore the full weight of his inability to do more than he did. What we really mean by these phrases like, "Rescue doesn't work," is, "Trying to save a life is only valid if we can succeed. It's not worth the effort if there is a chance of failure. I'm too small [for God to use]. God has a better way [than my sacrifice]. [People who try anyway make me feel bad for not trying, so] these guys must be crazy. [Because] I've tried [to save a life once or twice], I know what I'm talking about [and doing nothing (or doing *anything* else) is better than trying to save a life]." The weight of this self-pity is to say in effect, "Pity me for trying, failing, and never trying again. Do not pity the children who are now dead or the children who will die in the future because I'm not returning to the battle."

is done, or we are dead in our grave, if we are released, we are only released to Rescue again and again in God's kingdom.

Maybe you cannot rush out and stand today. Maybe you feel beaten, or that further effort is futile. Nonsense! If nothing else, you can begin to take steps to take that stand next year. You can begin to protect your property from lawsuits — or to get rid of it. But whatever you do with your belongings, you can seal your heart to God so that if they seize your property they will not seize your heart with it. You can begin to raise support. You can begin to disciple your church or family to stand with you. My Joshua is not unique. Your children would stand as tall as he did if you would let them, instead of shackling them with your own fear of obeying God disguised as prudence. You can adopt a missionary to the preborn, or take a second job and contribute it to the support of someone who is leaving everything. You can make a daily or weekly phone call to some tyrant judge somewhere and tell him to let God's people go that they may serve Him. You can discipline yourself to make that call until he lets them go. You can begin to set your affairs and priorities in order so that your whole life reflects God's answer to this (or any other) holocaust; so that your whole life becomes a window onto the reality of what is happening in the American womb; so that your whole life resounds with the Gospel.

Brutality and injustice toward us raise the question: "Will you stand with the children and so become a window to their world of torture and death?" or, "Will you stand with the world and cooperate with those who protect their killers?" The hardness of society's heart, the Church's heart, and even our own hearts, makes us realize that we are not prepared to become that window; and so we must ask: "What are we doing today that will make us ready to stand with them two or three years from now?" The need is not going away. Will we still be using the same old excuses for not standing then?

The Church will stand. Why am I so confident in this? Because God has made two promises: first, that He will not be left without a witness; and second, that those who will not be His witnesses, cannot be His people. That means, *someone* will stand.

But it also asks the ultimate question, *Will it be you?*

"Do not think," Mordecai reminded his adopted daughter Esther,

> that because you are in the king's house, you of all the Jews will escape. For if you remain silent at this time, relief and deliverance for the Jews will come from another place, but you and your father's family will perish. And who knows but that you have come to royal position for such a time as this?[6]

Your broken body, your life poured out, may be the only view our generation has, not only into the womb, but onto the Cross itself.

You know God is calling you. Begin now to answer as you can, and prepare for that coming day when you can answer fully.

---

[6] Esther 4:12-14.

Chapter 7

INTOLERANCE:
THE ENMITY OF THE CROSS

I know your deeds, and your love and faith and service and perseverance, and that your deeds of late are greater than at first. But this I have against you, that you tolerate the woman Jezebel . . . . Behold I will cast her upon a bed of sickness, and those who commit adultery with her into great tribulation, unless they repent of her deeds.

Revelation 2:20,22

What Does It Mean to Be Intolerant?

I had this neighbor, see, and my wife couldn't tolerate his loud music. So I suggested: "You can block it out of your mind; argue with him; make friends and convert him to your kind of music (or just get him to play his quietly); lobby for a noise ordinance; threaten his (or his dog's) life; throw a rock through his window; picket his house; destroy his hi-fi; move away; or shoot him (or his dog). Which one will effectively win his heart and end his loud invasion?" To which she answered, "Do we really want to win his heart? A lot of those other things sounded like more fun."

We spend much of our lives trying to match the appropriate level of intolerance to the many things that we should not tolerate. Intolerance conveys a closed-mindedness, putting you beyond investigation and discussion on the matter. It puts you in a frame of mind to take action, to bring to an end whatever it is you are intolerant of. The key concept of intolerance is "eliminate." *In a word, intolerance is the opposite of choice.*

Four Expressions of Intolerance

1) *Symbolic Intolerance.* If you are intolerant of ideas, you can close your mind against them, be rude about them, speak, publish, and publicly demonstrate against them. This is the battle of one idea against another.

2) *Positive intolerance.* Instead of eliminating what we cannot endure, we can provide alternatives to it. Prohibitionists, for instance, installed drinking fountains in the work place and on street corners so that sheer thirst would not be an excuse for a man to take to drink.

3) *Physical intolerance of things.* If you are physically in tolerant of "things," such as nukes or beer, you will attempt to neutralize them physically. Of course, you want to make them illegal, but in the meantime you want to do things that will both protect society from them and move others to take their threat seriously.

4) *Physical intolerance of people.* By physically hurting or killing the people who do them or create them, you eliminate the things and actions you cannot tolerate. For instance, in 1989 a woman planted a remote control land-mine next to the parking place of the chairman of a large corporation which was involved in animal experimentation. Apartheid and Jim Crow laws are particularly odious forms of lawful intolerance directed physically toward people in a minority group. The ANC, race riots, and the reverse discrimination of quota laws — today's form of preferential policies — are similarly odious forms of intolerance directed toward the people in the majority. One socially accepted form of physical intolerance against people might be beating up a child molester. While not officially countenanced, few juries would convict you, even if urged to by attorneys from the ACLU and MORAL, the Molesters' Rights Action League.

Who Is Intolerant in the Abortion Wars?

Pro-lifers fear being called "intolerant" about as much as we fear any name they could throw at us. This is because we have confused mercy and kindness with toleration. We want to be kinder than Jesus. Often kindness is the exact opposite of toleration. Failure to apply appropriate intolerance toward the bad behavior of children can be deadly not only for the child, but for a whole society, as King David found out with Absalom, and as permissive America is discovering.

It is time we understand what intolerance is and how we can express it effectively to drive child-killing back to hell. We must lead our society and Church to be as intolerant of child-killing and those who defend it as they are of Nazi war crimes and those who defend them.

I am intolerant of child-killing, of child-killers, of the police and political systems which protect child-killers, of a society which encourages child-killers, and of a Church which tolerates the whole lot of them. I think you should be too. I think we need to express our intolerance in a way which appropriately reflects God's intolerance to each of these facets of the growing abortion culture. But I am amazed that so many people are afraid of being called intolerant when the accusation comes from perhaps the most intolerant people on the earth: abortion advocates — who should be thankful that we take our cue from Proverbs 24:11 instead of from Exodus 21:24.

Go through the four kinds of intolerance with respect to how abortion advocates treat the children they do not want:

1) *They are symbolically intolerant* by calling them "fetuses," "products of conception," or "parasites;" calling the murder a "termination," or "surgical procedure;" calling us "violent" when we picket, and "emotional" when we argue.

2) *They express no positive intolerance* of children — they have never provided alternatives for women who bear their children and need help — because even more intolerable to them than pregnancy is motherhood. What they try to pass off as their three "positive" solutions to children are contraception — preventing children from even existing in the first place; government welfare — forced wealth redistribution; and public day-care programs — surrogate parenting by the government. Most fight personal charity and biological parenting because they are so hardened against children that they cannot imagine that anyone else — even a mother — might be capable of simple compassion. See how they fight adoption!

3) *They show physical intolerance of things* by painting signs on the Supreme Court steps and defacing office buildings which hold pro-life organizations.

4) *They show their physical intolerance of people* by bodily attacking Rescuers, throwing AIDS-infested urine and sperm on them, often beating and biting them until bloody. But most

pointedly, they show ultimate physical intolerance of people by terminating children they have no use for with what terrorists and the CIA call "extreme prejudice."

Regardless of how intolerant or violent any Christian might become, he will never come close to practicing the kinds of intolerance abortionists practice 4,500 times a day. If Christians treated abortionists with the same level of intolerance that abortionists treat their victims, it would only take half a day to run out of abortionists.

Another way to put the pro-life movement's tolerance into perspective is to compare it to other social movements. Pro-lifers have never rioted, looted, or burned down sections of town as in the sixties. More property damage was caused in the 1986 campus demonstrations against apartheid than in all abortion clinic bombings put together since 1973. Compare also the harshness with which pro-lifers are treated: the average bomber gets ten to twenty years of prison; the rioters of the sixties got suspended sentences. First-time Rescuers can get six months.

This Present Darkness

It is important to put even the most violent aspect of the pro-life track record into perspective. If you listen to the abortion culture, you can easily get the impression that pro-lifers generally, and Rescuers in particular, are hate-filled, violent, and abusive liars. Much of the Church is emerging from a sixty-year cultural sleep to hear all of these accusations willingly portrayed by the press. "Surely," they think, "if the police say Christians assaulted them and even charge someone with a felony,[1] there must be some substance to it. When the child-killing advocates say that picketers, sidewalk counselors, and crisis pregnancy center workers are rude and abusive — would they lie?"

This phenomenon of bald-faced lies on the part of the child-

---

[1] Usually the *felony* is a charge of conspiracy to commit a *misdemeanor*. Of course they never put down the formal charge this way for all to laugh at their patent absurdity. But in California I was twice charged with such a felony. In both cases the title of the charge was "Conspiracy to Corrupt Public Morals." While not as romantic as my Washington, D.C., charges of "Incommoding," or as whimsical as a 6 month sentence in Toledo for "Loitering," it still had the ring of the ridiculous to it.

killers and the willingness of the public to believe them is most disturbing. I have three explanations for the darkness which cloaks their lies and the Church's unwillingness to penetrate this present darkness:

1) *The concept of abortion, itself, is fundamentally inhuman.* Abortion violates everything that men and women are at the core of their being. To uncover it in its stark reality is more than the soul can bear. Any lie, any covering, is preferable. The guilt runs so deep that many mothers coming to kill their young, and the staff who assist her, really think they hear abusive names when in fact all that is going on is one young woman offering a mother help, saying, "Let us help you." Their own guilt abuses them. They must flee it.

2) *The act of child murder is the epitome of mindless violence.* The image of a mother holding her child still while the hands of a physician, trained in healing, stalk her helpless child to dismember it for money defies explanation — it must be hidden. We will accept any lie about those who expose it if only we can redraw the veil of ignorance over it.

3) *Knowing that this is taking place publicly in our towns and neighborhoods makes us fellow conspirators.* Such knowledge is too terrible to contemplate. It cannot be true! Splatter movies — *The Texas Chainsaw Massacres*, Jason, and Freddie Krueger — come close to portraying the reality of innocence stalked by evil. If abortion is what our entire society knows in its heart that it must be, then we have unleashed a Jason or Freddie into our neighborhoods. It just cannot be!

This mass hysteria stops at nothing to hide its nightmare, even projecting its own sin onto the pro-life movement. They cannot bear to think of what they have done in the name of freedom, career, sex, love, and personal rights. Intolerance, violence, rudeness, lack of love and compassion — this is abortion. Yet, listening to the media you would think that it is those seeking to protect the unborn who are guilty of violence. You might imagine it easy to convince people that this insanity of tearing babies limb from limb must stop. But insanity listens only to its own twisted, guilty logic. Those who could stop it are stunned by the awesome reality they have permitted to grow up alongside them. It cannot be true! We must not let it be true. And so we turn our backs and pretend that it is not true.

Psychiatrists and counselors have often noted the phenomenon of the mother who willfully blinds herself to her husband's sexual molestation of her children. She will do anything to hold her family together. Though she "sees" what is going on, she refuses to perceive it. Facing the consequences of exposing the reality of what is happening to her children and family is more horrible to her than the reality of her husband's perversion — and so rather than protect them, she continues to let them be devoured.

It is not unusual for a wife in these circumstances to project the very things she is hiding onto those who disturb her illusions. Any lie will do to cover her sense of shame. She will physically attack anyone who threatens her dream world — including her own children who are seeking to escape. Is this insanity? Welcome to the Church in America; the land where thirty million children were publicly murdered in sight of at least fifty million people who believe that it is murder. Yet, not only did they do next to nothing to stop it, they attacked anyone who tried to expose it or protect her children.

Can you see why all solutions which lack in principle the element of physical intolerance will never generate the moral force to pierce the layered veil of shadowed conspiracy shrouding this cancer? The evil is too great. Our guilt overwhelms us. *We do not want to know. We will attack whoever tries to tell us.* **We will attack anyone who shows us that there is something we can do to prevent it.** *We cannot afford even to support Rescuers. They expose our nakedness.* This is why any activity which does not deal directly with and overcome our fear of the reality of abortion will never arouse people to penetrate the veil of evil darkness which protects child-killing today. This is why we must be actively intolerant.

Piercing the Darkness

We usually think of intolerance in terms of narrow-minded people who are obnoxious to others for insignificant reasons. But there are a number of things *demanding* intolerance: rape, bigotry, wife and child abuse, to name a few. If it is right to be intolerant of these, then intolerance in and of itself is not wrong. The question is, *"What should we be actively intolerant of; what should we physically prevent others from choosing to do?"*

Some people say that the law should be their guide. Some have even made an absolute moral principle along these tolerant lines: "What the law permits (or tolerates), we permit." This principle is dangerously useless for anything, let alone helping someone think through Rescue. It is useless because it is nothing more than a description of what we normally do. It is dangerous because it deceives us into thinking that what we normally do is a moral principle to guide what we *ought* to do.

It is not enough to determine whether or not something is legally or socially permitted. We have to ask whether or not it is something which God allows us to permit. Of course the law might permit something. We want to know if God will permit us to join in that sin by obeying that law.

Does God allow us to tolerate or permit child-killing? I submit to you that the chief reason any of us would say "Yes" is that saying "No" would cost us too much.[2] It is not surprising that Proverbs 24:11, "Rescue those dragged to the slaughter," is introduced with the words: "If you faint in the day of adversity, how small your strength is." Bold as a lion in our dreams, we imagine ourselves with Corrie ten Boom in occupied Holland, and Richard Wurmbrandt in solitary confinement in the Gulag. We just know that we would protect Jews and preach the Gospel no matter the cost. Yet we do not have the courage to speak out when ethnic slurs are cast, and most of us have not shared the Gospel with anyone in the last three months, much less preached it to people who threaten us harm if we continue to bring them the claims of the Most High God.

So with Peter we say, "I will never forsake Thee, Lord!" And yet, in the day of adversity, the Church lets IRS 501(c)3 tax exemption dictate what we preach. We let the Supreme Court determine where we pray. We let the child-killing trespass law determine our commitment to life. We let the suburbs determine where we live. We forgot that Jesus gave a very simple formula

---

[2] I Kings 20:11.

for our love and concern for Him: "Inasmuch as you [actually]
did it to the least of these My little ones, you have done it unto
Me. . . . For whoever is ashamed of Me and My words in this
adulterous and sinful generation, the Son of Man will also be
ashamed of him when He comes in the Glory of His Father with
the holy angels."[3] What would you do for Jesus the King of
the Universe? Probably as much as you do for the children
crying out to you today for protection. *Hitler never required the
common people to kill Jews. He merely required them to permit
him to kill them.* Hitler, Planned Parenthood, the ACLU, the
NOW, the NEA, and your local abortionist — all they ask is
your toleration, in effect, your permission.

So how active should our intolerance to child-killing be?
Surely we need a symbolic form of intolerance: it must include
a philosophical and theological dimension in addition to visible
demonstrations, protests, and lobbying. We should be providing
positive intolerance in our alternatives to murder — crisis
pregnancy centers, mom's houses, shepherding homes, chastity-
based sex education. Because it is murder, we should be willing
to sympathize with and be unashamed of those whose intolerance
to child-killing leads them to destroy the abortion death camps
even though we ourselves do not do this. But we must do more
than just penetrate the darkness with good activities. More than
anything else, we must shine the light of physical intolerance
toward abortion/murder — that intolerant light shining directly
from the Cross of Christ — our pattern is the light of His
intolerance of a world of sin. It shines far clearer, unobscured
by the smoke of politicians' promises. It does more to warm the
heart of a people than the heat generated when a death camp
burns down at night, as warm as that glow is for the children
scheduled to be killed the next day. To pierce the darkness of
the night we must be willing to actively oppose it. To shatter
that dark we must physically oppose it with the Cross.

Shattering the Darkness

By focusing the Gospel at the heart of the death industry
itself, Rescue incorporates the necessary level of intolerance

---

[3] Matthew 25:40,45; Mark 8:31-38; Luke 9:22-26; I Samuel 2:30.

which allows each of the other elements of the solution to child-killing to be most effective. As Judi Brown pointed out on the *Operation Rescue Video*, each Rescue is a capsule of the entire pro-life movement — compassionate counseling, offering alternatives, creating the basis for a legal challenge to *Roe v. Wade* in the courts, making a political statement, giving politicians a platform on which to take action, personally involving a cross-section of the community, and reviving churches through a deep affirmation of the core of Judeo-Christian faith in a God who saves, who intervenes, who Rescues — all this just by trying to physically save a baby's life.

The physical intolerance of the Cross uncovers the child-killing conspiracy in our society root and branch. The persecution of Rescuers by every level of government shows that child-killing is not an isolated phenomenon. It is not just "permitted;" it is enforced by every level of our democratic/republican institutions which have become like gods to us. The Cross reveals the true heart of organizations such as the National Education Association, the Democratic Party (and many Republicans), old-line "Christian" denominations which still think of themselves as "main-line," the entire American penal and justice system, not to mention Planned Parenthood, People for the American Way, and the American Civil Liberties Union. The persecution of Rescuers, so blandly permitted by the Church, shows how much of the Church is hopelessly wed to the treasures of Egypt, lusting after Babylonian officers painted on the walls of our temples.[4]

The power of Rescue is the power of the principles of the Cross, building on repentance for our toleration of child-killing, and a commitment to refuse to tolerate it. When you rescue, God physically intervenes through your life laid down for your neighbor — not just the unborn neighbor, but laid down for the abortionist, the police, the judges, and our fellow Christians who look the other way. When the Church becomes characterized by the light of this kind of love, it will finally shatter the darkness, and the darkness will never overcome it. This should not be sur-

---

[4] Hebrews 11:25-26; Ezekiel 23:14-21.

prising, since repentance leading to healing is the keynote of the Church. It is what Jesus died to establish, rose again to secure, and sent his Spirit to empower.

In the Cross God showed forth His utter intolerance of sin, and His supreme intolerance of a fallen creation. In Rescue we show forth that same intolerance by paying a part of the price for bringing healing. How do Christians "kill" the abortionist, or "destroy" his clinic? By laying down our lives for him, when we stand in solidarity with those he would murder, as Christ stood in our place two thousand years ago.

Chapter 8

PROPHET, KING, PRIEST: THE WAY OF THE CROSS

The chief divisions among Rescuers are usually thought to run along the lines of how far one should or should not go to refuse cooperation with the legal system. The arguments consuming them become as arcane to outsiders as three rabbis arguing over a Midrash. They split hairs over where and how to draw the line: We go limp until we get to the paddy wagon, but then we walk; or we go limp in jail except to make a phone call; or we will walk out of our cells into a common room, but never back into our cells.

When dealing with Rescue, it is hard to speak to the technical issues and yet remain intelligible, readable, and pertinent to a broader audience. To some, the parts of this book dealing with the details of what happened to Operation Rescue are fascinating. For others, they seem pointless — "Get on with it!" I can hear you say. "Is there anything in these arguments which is generally pertinent to all Christians?"

Yes, these arguments are typical of Christian discussions in every realm of life where compromise with the world is an issue. If you look closely, it is the king and the prophet arguing — the king pointing out how there are no pure actions, therefore we must *always* make a calculated tradeoff; the prophet, seeking to find a way to be utterly consistent, knows that there *must* be a way! And the priest is looking ahead to be sure that what we produce will indeed be a transforming intercession as opposed to either prophetic suicide or simply replacing their oppressive king with ours. Very often hostility will break out because the kingly way seems like hopeless compromise to the prophet, and the prophetic life seems like blind suicide to the king. And to these two the priest just seems preachy, because "Of course we kings and prophets want *true* transformation, so why, Priest, do you keep nagging us to keep our sights fixed on heart-change?"

If you understand this, then you can see that the arguments

101

within Rescue are a microcosm of the Christian walk. We all want to live consistently like Christ with integrity and no compromise. And yet we seek to be wise and not alienate people, choosing carefully where and when we go to the wall. The issue in this book is abortion, but the principles we debate come from any part of your life where to live in peace the world requires you to live by its standards rather than God's.

KING: You've painted yourself into a corner.

PROPHET: How so?

KING: By declaring that you will stand with the children in your city at any cost. You have set up your battle lines so that there is no escape to go do something else, without appearing to abandon the babies. And you can't go on rescuing if you spend all your time in jail. What's worse, your strong stand has left no one willing to stand with you either in or out of jail!

PROPHET: You make it sound as if this is some new problem we face. Didn't we get involved in Rescue precisely *because* Church and society had already abandoned the babies? We knew from the beginning that wherever we proved ourselves serious about standing with the babies, society would go to any lengths to make sure the babies stay abandoned. So they broke us in the city where Operation Rescue first drew a line in the sand, and now we see the pattern of that city being reproduced around the nation — wherever mass Rescues have seriously challenged child-killing, the city quickly finds our price and we go home. Isn't this just the price of not abandoning the children: that we be faithful to what we said we would do?

KING: Not at all. The purpose of Rescue is to do it where it works. If you don't have church support; if the city keeps you in jail so that your actual rescuing is almost nil; then it's time to shake the dust off your feet against that city and go where you can be effective.

PROPHET: What you mean is, "Go where we do not have to prove that God is worth obeying at any cost; go where we can continue our activism unchallenged and only *talk* as if we would pay any price; hope that enough people pump up enough excitement to make it look as if we mean business when we challenge the system; pray they never call our bluff."

KING: Well, what do you want to do: stand with the children or sit in jail?

PROPHET: That's a false dilemma. If you are in jail for saving a child's life, then you are standing with *that* child. *He* could never have been saved had you not stood with *him* for the three to six month jail sentence. Besides, you surely are not saying that children who can be saved without big sentences are worth protecting, but those who require long jail time are not?

KING: I am simply saying that you would rather sit in jail than save babies.

PROPHET: No, it goes much deeper than that. It really comes down to the fact that I don't want to become a Rescue activist *outside* the Church, organizing a crusade which will succeed with or without the Lord sending revival to His people. In other words, I don't see "organization" as the key issue. I see the keys of the kingdom lying in the hands of the people God has already organized — His Church — as they become what He intended: a living sacrifice.

KING: Well, sitting in jail certainly won't further that goal. All you do is demoralize the Church by calling it to become some kind of kamikaze. The fact is, I'm the one who is truly interested in seeing the Church mobilized. That is why I try to develop wise strategies which take into account our weaknesses and don't turn people off up front by demanding that they do — right *now!* — things they do not have the strength or vision to do at this time. So we pick battles and set the terms of them very carefully. Victory is important.

PROPHET: Yes, but the only road to victory is to die to yourself. At first perhaps, people might think that I am making a suicidal call to action. But in time, after they have been burned by the broken promises of enthusiastic uprising, dashed against the rocks of a city determined to crush any movement of people who are not prepared to die — sooner or later, they will flock to moral integrity, because only moral integrity will prepare people to pay the price of bringing lasting change. America's problem — Church, Society, and State — is not that it needs more organizing, more information, and 10% more pro-life voters. We need men and women who are 100% intolerant of child murder whether it is legal or illegal. We need such people to stand with the children whether they stand with the children at the death camps and in jail, in the Crisis Pregnancy Centers, or in the halls of political power. Rescuers in West Hartford and California prove that it is worth being viciously beaten to protect children. Rescuers in Baton Rouge and Wichita prove that when arrested it is worth walking rather than going limp if it gets the police to help protect children. Rescuers in Milwaukee prove that it is worth rescuing every day to protect children. Rescuers in Atlanta prove that it is worth sitting in jail for months only to be released to rescue again and again.

KING: Look. My goal is revival: thousands of people filled with the resolution to go down and end the killing. If enough go, then there will be far too many moving at once for the city or abortionist to deal with.

PROPHET: Revival? Isn't it when we are completely helpless that God moves? Then everyone can see that it is not by our might or power, but through His Spirit enabling us to pay the price of obedience — to withstand any penalty rather than cling to the things of this earth as the pagans do. It is the example of the few which will motivate generations. We must find those few, raise them up, and support them.

KING: "Few" is the word for it! You want people to rescue and lose their houses too? That's what I mean about your having painted yourself into a corner. Who's going to join you? "The few" will not spark an uprising. All your strategy will do is alienate everyone with your rhetoric, and scare them off with the punishments you get from court.

PROPHET: What do you mean "my" rhetoric? What I am saying is no different from what all Operation Rescue leaders said in '88 and '89. Was it true then? When did it change? They're *not* killing babies? There really *is* a political solution which will save a child scheduled to die *today*? If so, why did we call for *Rescue* instead of *politics* back in '88? Suffering service is no longer the call of the Church? We *should* allow fear of man's punishments to stop us today, but not in '88?

KING: You're in a small corner, so you condemn whoever doesn't join you. Shake the dust off your feet and come out.

PROPHET: If I "shake the dust from my feet" as you say, I would be shaking it off against myself as much as I would be shaking it against the Christians of this city who have turned their backs on the children. *By leaving I would be just as guilty of abandoning the children of this city as they are.* Talk about self-righteous, I'm not made more righteous than my brothers by going to where it's easy to save a life. In the end it's the children of this city who must pay for my self-righteous act of dust-shaking. I'm here because where the opposition is greatest and we are the weakest is where God can do the most. Is this just theory, or is it strategic fact?

KING: I'll tell you what it is. It's pride. You can't admit that you failed and let God start fresh in your life, and so you keep banging your head against a wall. If people won't join you (because it's impossible to) then you'll go to jail and hold your breath until you turn blue. That tactic will never work except to give you a warm feeling inside that you were tough. Why can't you work for something that *can* take hold and change society? Someday there will be a national Rescue somewhere. It will begin like Atlanta and Wichita, only instead of shrinking back, the Church will surge forward and experience true revival and it will spread around the country.

PROPHET: Of course, but this will not happen until Christians have come to grips sufficiently with the enormous size of the cost of discipleship. Sooner or later, jail or worse is the price for standing with the children. There is no easy city, because every city and most of the Christians in them have been trained to worship law and order *at any cost.* Though they will begin with liking the idea of "ending child-killing by Rescue," they will love man's law, order, personal peace, and prosperity more. When the legal system of any city decides to take Rescue seriously, the Christians will fall back, *unless and only unless there is Revival.* Therefore, the only way to succeed is to raise up a generation of people who will lay down their lives.

KING: See? You're condemning those who can't rescue all the time — who aren't a part of your "raised-up" generation.

PROPHET: Are you intentionally missing the point? You are the one who condemns those who don't rescue, not I. You condemn them by telling me to shake the dust off my feet against

them just because of some long jail sentences.   But the Bible
says that it is when we are finally willing to face any earthly
threat, that God has us where He wants us, and the enemy where
He wants them.   As long as there are Rescuers on the street, or
political action, or demonstrations, there is a sense that someone
is out there who can get the job done.   Jail changes that.   When
we go to jail, then the true inability and helplessness of the
Church becomes clear to all.   We bear in jail a final witness to
our inability, and throw ourselves on God's ability to act.

KING: Look, I respect your determination, but it's foolish.
We need to take back the power bases of society, not flee to the
ascetic wilderness of jail.   We said this from the beginning of
Operation Rescue, even though people like you have a selective
memory.   I fear for you.   Of course political activism is not to
become an end in itself.   It is to take back the power bases — to
heal.   *But you forget all this.   You would rather sit in jail and let
babies die for generations than get elected and change the law.
We are not going to change Western civilization by sitting in
front of the door of a clinic.*   We must take back the power bases
we have abandoned.   People just aren't going to respond to
abortion any more.   They need to see their self-interest in the
broader issues abortion touches.   Turning to politics is not
bailing out.   You don't have to paint yourself into a corner and
make Rescue a sacrament.

PROPHET: Don't mock the Cross by making it sound as if
I'm saying that only sit-ins are taking up the Cross.   Sitting-in
at an abortion clinic is not the end-all of Christian faith — dying
to self and living for Christ is.   The sit-in is not the sacrament.
The Cross is simply its pattern.   As for the idea of getting
elected, if I am not elected from jail, then the country has not
changed enough to make me useful in office; they would eat me
alive if I ever got there.   I don't object your political call.   In
fact, I believe that kingly types must be kept out of jail.   All
they do there is pace around driving everyone crazy with ideas
of how they could change the world if it weren't for these walls
of concrete and steel holding them in.   But keep me out of
politics.   All I'd do is pace around and drive everyone crazy
with my ideas about how I could serve the Lord if I weren't
confined by the walls of political expedience.   And perhaps in

this we only exhibit our sin — you in your calculated inconsistency and me in my vain consistency. But hear this, the only thing that makes my position a "corner" or a "trap" is that to remain true to our words — *our* words mind you, we both say, "Abortion is murder and we will act like it" — to remain true, we may have to pay a huge price, you in your political office and I in my prison cell. To you, this looming "price" is your greatest corner or trap. For me, it is our greatest opportunity. I do not object to your politicking to become king. I simply warn you not to be a king like the other nations.

KING: You warn me? Take heed yourself that you do not judge whoever doesn't join you. When you fail to draw a crowd, don't justify your failure by sucking in God knows how many "missionaries" to fail with you and point their fingers and talk about Gideon, and weakness being strength. It was *God* who told Gideon to get rid of all those men, it wasn't a death wish on the part of Gideon. Look at how many cities Paul and Silas ran away from. Fight the battle wisely! Brother, I say this because I love you, yet I fear for you and your arrogant pride. Don't lose the war because you are too pig-headed to take a step back and gather some who are less bold than you.

PROPHET: Paul was run *out* of a lot of cities, but he never let what a city might do to him keep him from going *into* it. Yet there came a day when he stopped running. But how can we begin to compare ourselves with Paul's example? When you've been beaten seven times, stoned three times, and spent three straight years in jail, then you can say, "Let's use Paul's more moderate and wise tactics!" If God's requirement was good enough for Gideon, then our Lord's example is good enough for me. He promised we would rule if we were fit to serve. He promised that we would be fit to live if we were willing to die in His name. He was offered all the kingdoms of this world if He would only rule them the way Satan wanted them to be ruled. Instead, He chose to serve and die for them — and behold, He now rules them. He never ran for office. He never called for the overthrow of Caesar. He never called for His people to seize the power bases through political muscle, only through humble excellence of service in every field of human endeavor which might constitute a power base. Yet His kingdom continues to spread across the earth — not at the edge of some sword which His people wield against the enemy, but where the enemy wields its sword against His people. Even today it brings down governments and empires which in this century have murdered 950 million of their citizens. They are coming down, not because Christians seize political power, but because they earned it through generations of Christians willing to die. Why should we change this way of life for a tactic that preserves our skins at the cost of making ourselves into the image of the one who offered our Lord all the kingdoms of the earth? It is by dying for what is right and true; it is by acting as Jesus would act, and doing so at any price, that we gather those who are less bold than ourselves. If we want the Church to take a step forward, then *we* must take a step forward — not a step back. I don't want to be any less "pig-headed" than my Lord. Were He not "pig-headed," as you say, He would never have gone to the Cross, and you and I would not be having this argument; we would be burning in the righteous judgments of hell. Yes, we'll rule as kings — but only in those arenas where we're willing to die as His servants. This is the Samaritan strategy. It is the way of the Cross.

PRIEST: I've not said anything until now because the priestly aspect of taking up the Cross is not in particular dispute. Most Rescuers seem willing to be so harmless in their inter-cession for the children that I wonder if they are non-violent not because of any desire to imitate our Lord, but rather their stark fear of being too bold in their defense of the little ones. But that is not what I wanted to say to you both.

This is your dilemma: You, Prophet, want a mass movement no less than the king, and you, Sire, no less than the prophet must have troops willing to pay any price. While seeming to deny the other, you actually affirm each other. You will never succeed alone, or by pretending that either of you is sufficient without the other.

For you, O King, the day will come when you must fight, and fight well. You cannot run forever. If you do not grasp your opportunities and risk everything, the timely moments will slip through your fingers and you will find yourself no longer building a movement, but sliding into irrelevance, all the while telling yourself that you are saving yourself and your troops for the next battle. If you ever do seriously engage the child-killing forces, you will do serious jail time, you will probably see marriages ruined, jobs and houses lost, and much harm come to the physical well-being of those who stand with the children.

But Prophet, take that smug smile off your face! I know you have already lost home and job, and that some of you have lost families as well. But if God blesses your sacrifice, you will be successful. Many will follow your path, and much wisdom in leading them will be absolutely required. Without it, your own pig-headedness will alienate the very ones you must lead in order to succeed in transforming Church and nation. Your principles are what guide you. Beware that you do not permit children to die so that you can cling like a pharisee to your principles. Each in your own way is playing politics with your principles, with the lives of children, and Rescuers. Now is the time for humility and teamwork before it is too late to make a lasting change in the West for many centuries.

PROPHET and KING: Who asked you?

PRIEST: Your endless bickering invites reproof. Isn't it obvious to you by now that neither of you can succeed alone? Neither of you is fit to bring change.

PROPHET and KING: But I don't trust him!

PRIEST: Did I hear you two right? Even though you agree on ninety-five percent, that five percent is more important to you than the life of a child? You are an embarrassment, and a disgrace, both of you! If you cannot work together, then you have nothing to offer the divided house of Beelzebub but the rhetoric of your father below.

KING: Well, he's always trying to turn every Rescue into Armageddon, and usually my skin's the prize of war. Since I have the visibility, I'm the one who's pushed first toward the bullets. Besides, he's so narrow he destroys our credibility with the broader groups. He . . .

PROPHET: Me? Look who's always picking a fight in some city with Armageddon rhetoric, and about the time anyone's ready to treat it like a serious stand for the children, you pack up and go home. I can't trust you to stand your ground.

PRIEST: Yes, yes, of course. As I said, you're too busy fighting each other again as usual. You don't even have sense enough to admit it and weep!

KING: I'm sorry. I just can't trust him; he undermines me.

PRIEST: If you will permit me, Sire, that's nonsense. The prophet doesn't undermine you, he merely takes your words literally and acts on them, expecting you to do the same — prophets are always assuming that he who is bold enough to speak is bold enough to do.

PROPHET: Well, Priest, you at least can see why I can't trust the king, he just doesn't stand behind his word.

PRIEST: I hate it when prophets whine! Of course you can trust the king, but first you must appreciate the difference between what he says as a leader and what he does as a strategic general. So quit talking about trust. Trust isn't the issue between you two, it's pure pride creating a tempest in the teapot of rescue-movement politics — the same way Christians do when they argue about church politics or national policy; the same way husbands and wives fight over foolish things; the same way children rebel by manipulating their parents.

Get to work instead. Call the Church to her historic task of reaching all the earth. Keep your goal in sight — it's not to topple society, but to transform it. We cannot force transformation, but we can lead in it by being a personal example. It will take both prophetic example and kingly planning to attract and motivate the hundreds of thousands to do what only *they* can do to be a part of this cleansing, transforming work. If you cannot work together, then we have nothing to offer the world; we are lost.

The Unique Task of the Church

While I have focused this dialogue on Rescue, can you see how it is simply two different parts of the Church talking about obedience to God? It could be in any arena. Wherever the rubber meets the road in the Christian life, Christians will argue this way. The *wise* course often seems cowardly, compromised and self-seeking; the course with *integrity* often seems hard-headed, harsh, suicidal, and judgmental. Where can wisdom and integrity unite? In the foolishness of the Cross. This is not only the heart of personal redemption, but of Christian ethics and of cultural dominion.

The issue is not politics vs direct action, or spirituality vs activism, or Church vs state, or even whether Christians in this dispensation should have anything to do with the kingdoms of this world. The issue is being faithful to lay down your life in all endeavors. If the rhetoric of the Cross paints us into a corner when it comes to rescuing babies at the abortion clinic, it is only because the rhetoric of the Cross should paint you into an equally intolerable corner when it comes to rescuing our political system; or loving a spouse who refuses to respond; or loving a pastor — or congregation — regardless of how bad they are to you; or giving a square deal to a customer no matter how offensive he is or how easy it would be to steal him blind — even if this customer is your own thieving irresponsible government. In all of these, or in taking back the power bases, it is the self-sacrificing service of the Cross which paints us into a corner. The world soothingly croons for us to just get along and do things its way, and stay out of the corner of its wrath. If we insist on obeying God, then the world stops crooning and by its threats backs us into that dread corner and hands us a cross — the same cross which Jesus keeps telling us to take up. If you are not in a corner where it is "refuse to serve God or die," then have you truly brought the claims of God's kingdom to a world which is dying without them? Whatever the kingly way might be, it is no short-circuit away from the Cross.

Christians are those who are being remade into the image of Jesus Christ. Those who take up the task to rescue either in front of the abortion clinic or in the political arena, dare not short-circuit that process. If we do, then should we ever seize the power bases of society — or the power base of home and Church — we will be as unfit to rule as those from whom we seized them. This is as true on the personal level of dealings between children, parents, wives, and husbands as it is on the level of culture, nation, and church. As Christ was Prophet, Priest, and King, so Christians have legitimate reason to reflect His ministry in these ways. His Kingship is the pattern of our political activity. It is real political activity, real authority, and real rule, based on the integrity of suffering service. Any other pattern for victory, though effective in the short term, will have the flaws for its own destruction built into it.

Everything we do must point to Jesus Christ. He is the pattern for the Church as she engages in politics, business, evangelism, and deeds of love and mercy. It is, of course, the pattern of Rescue. The power to serve is the power to rule. The power to lay down your life for another is what builds the moral capital to change hearts — even those hearts initially offended. It is the only soil where sound laws governing any country can grow.

Daniel is a model here. He understood the true threat to his ability to rule wisely. It was not the lion's den which would destroy him, but his failure to obey God. To cling to his political achievements and the "good he could do if only he remained in office" would be to give his enemies a far greater victory than they could have dreamed of. They just wanted him dead. But his true adversary, the devil, wanted his soul in compromise. Yes, Daniel would go to heaven even if he compromised, but he would leave the earth far worse than he found it. Until we have men and women of this caliber, we will never take back the power bases of any society. When we do have such people, we will not take the power bases back by conquest; rather, a thirsty people, choking to death on humanist sawdust, will turn to follow those who do all things well. We will inherit the power bases from the corruption of those who now consume them. Why should we take as our pattern the kings, priests, fathers, and citizens of the earth and those who rule the various power bases of society? Why do we want to rule our selves, our societies, our families and our Churches their way? We look for a new heaven and a new earth. We look to rule according to God's pattern. Therefore, we lay down our lives — we rescue.

SECTION III

THE CROSS

AND OPERATION RESCUE

"You will find," says the abortion culture, "that you cannot help but agree with our fundamental premise, which is, 'There can never be any difference between the hungers of the flesh, and the will of God.' You watch. We will show you that in reality you are on our side, despite what you say. Just look at yourself: you will stop rescuing in order to surround yourself with the same comforts of the flesh we surround ourselves with. You call it God's will that your fleshly comforts — or rescue organizations, or churches, or special ministries — be preserved even if it means that you must permit these little ones to die *today*. And that is what we say about abortion and preserving the opportunity of the woman to surround herself with equal comforts, even if it means that her child must die today."

The day of the Rescue rally is past. It is now time to do what we said we would do at all those rallies — and do not expect the cheering to continue when God uses you to answer Satan's challenge.

Chapter 9

THE CROSS
AND THE PRO-LIFE MOVEMENT

"If I Were Pro-choice, You'd Be Dead!"

In November of 1989, realizing the threat that Rescue posed to their right to choose, the pro-death factions rallied the largest crowd they had ever mustered, to run head to head with our first National Rescue in Washington, D.C. Jeff White, Western Regional Director of Operation Rescue, a few others, and I, put on our Operation Rescue T-shirts and walked into the crowd of 100,000. We managed to get within a hundred feet of Molly Yard on the steps of the Lincoln Memorial, as she thundered on about how bearing children is the ultimate slavery of women, from which they must be liberated. Then the police threw us out of this historic gathering for wearing pro-life T-shirts.

As we were driving away in Jeff's full-size pickup truck, he accelerated toward a mob of satisfied feminists crossing the street, and slammed on his brakes — screeching to a halt within inches of the scattering crowd. Sticking his head out the window he bellowed, "If I were pro-choice, you'd be dead now!"

This might horrify the delicate Christian, and confirm his suspicion that Rescuers really are out of control. But by slamming on his brakes instead of running them down, Jeff revealed a fundamental truth about how different he is — even when he is out of control — from those who advocate the choice to kill as a prime civil right. We are not pro-choice when it comes to killing people — if we were pro-choice, then baby-killing doctors and their supporters would be killed by the dozens. We must continue to let this anti-choice-to-murder position govern our hearts and emotions when we fit the various pro-life activities together.

The Litmus Test: Is It an Issue, or a Baby?

In the fifties and sixties abortion was an "issue" — some argued for it and some against it. But by 1973, it stopped being an issue and became a national fact. Those who believed that

115

killing the unborn was right were free to practice their faith.
Yet the Church, which believed it murder, was afraid to practice
its faith. The religion of MAN called people to murder children
cruelly to advance their own ends. Our walk with the living
God called us to protect the defenseless in spite of what it did to
advance or hinder our "ends." We treated our faith as if it were
theoretical. They have treated theirs as worth living by, even
worth sacrificing babies for. We have lost our credibility and
they have gained credibility, turning us into an abortion culture.
Those who boldly proclaim what they believe, *and then live consistently with it*, will gain credibility. They did. We did not.

When the Church finally did begin to get tentatively
involved in pro-life activities, we were very careful to make
them permit choice. By permitting it, we worshipped in
principle the "right" of the state to ordain murder, and the
"right" of the mother to kill. Every time there is a pro-life
activity carefully announced as "completely safe and legal,"
remember who first seized those words — those who want *safe*
sex, and the feminists who demand *safe, legal* abortion. When
the Church makes a cardinal virtue out of being respectably safe
and legal in the eyes of a decadent, murdering world, it is
sliding on a spiritual condom and going forth to a sterilized faith
with only the appearance of fruitful vigor.[1]

It is ironic that intervening to save children is in need of
lengthy defense among those who believe that abortion is
murder. To confine ourselves to activities which man finds
"legitimate" or "legal" inevitably confines us to building our

---

[1] Revelation 17:1-6. Since John is not talking about literal acts of sex
between the Harlot and the kings of the earth, what engages them in
fornication with her is their conformity to her idea of law. There comes
a time when you either fornicate with the kings of the earth and the Great
Harlot by obeying their laws, or you disobey their laws and become a
martyr — a witness by your death or imprisonment that God, not man, is
true. According to Acts 5:29, the issue requiring your life can be *any*
issue where the kings of the earth and God have made conflicting decrees:
"We must obey God rather than men." But not the American Church.
Through the wonders of modern spiritual prophylactics, we have
discovered how to have safe, legal fornication with these same kings of the
earth who fill the Harlot's cup (v 6) with the blood of the faithful (cf.
Ezekiel 23).

anti-murder programs on a commitment to permit murder. A house divided against itself cannot stand — and so far, the Church has not stood very convincingly in our generation for anything but her own worldly interests.

The litmus test for whether or not we have made compromise a principle of our pro-life activities is our reaction to Rescue. Wherever Rescue is supported, compromise is only tactical. Where it is opposed, the right to choose has become a way of life, a principle.

*How is Rescue the litmus test? Because the other pro-life weapons, while working to achieve their objective, must meanwhile permit the choice to kill. Rescue is the one activity which, while it is being carried out, does not permit choice. Did Rescuers dream up this test to condemn nonrescuers? Not at all. All pro-lifers have the same goal: **End** choice in the realm of child murder. Though the idea still seems radical to some, we need to see that it is the political activist, the educator, the crisis pregnancy center administrator, the preacher, who must justify how they can engage in activities which do not challenge the basic assumption that **today** we must leave a woman free to kill, if she so chooses.*

Please hear me. People involved in these activities should no more feel that I am being critical of them here, than a military doctor should feel criticized because he is not carrying a gun. Tactically, some pro-life activities *must* permit choice. The nature of the activity demands it. But this does not mean that those involved in these other activities must make it a principle to oppose Rescue, or that those not sitting-in should be afraid of defending and cheering for those who do. We must support legal, intellectual, moral, *and* physical intolerance of murder, regardless of what our own part in ending it might be.

Each area of pro-life activity becomes vital to an over-all solution only as it reflects the pattern of the Cross. The fundamental question is not, "Did you do a sit-in?" Rather, it is: "What are you doing sacrificially to protect your neighbor; to honor God; to be like Jesus?"

Rescue at an abortion clinic is the only way to take up your cross on behalf of those whose mothers have passed by every opportunity to change their minds, and are now — at this moment — entering the death camp itself. *But it is not the only way to take up your cross, either in the anti-abortion ministry of the Church, or in your broader life as a Christian.* This is extremely important to understand, because many Christians have done much damage by misrepresenting Rescue at this point. There is no one form of ministry which has an arm-lock on living as Christ would live. The pattern of the Cross is applicable to every arena, whether in the anti-abortion movement or in any other area of the Christian life.

It should be obvious that the Cross is to pattern every way a Christian lives. The simple fact that it is in vogue for all parts of the pro-life world to call their activity "Rescue," is a telling proof of this. The unique importance of Rescue is that it directly withdraws our cooperation with the murder of those children for whom all other efforts have failed. To find the unique importance of Rescue no more threatens the importance of every other pro-life activity, than the unique necessity of other pro-life actions should make it unnecessary to block the doors of a death camp for those 4,500 children a day whose mothers will not listen to any other argument.

The Whole Body of Christ

We need many parts of the body to address legalized murder, because what we do must reflect the differences between child-killing in the womb and other forms of brutal physical assault. First, the mother — the mother herself — is willing to go along with it, and usually to finance it. Second, the Church — the Church herself — has degenerated to the point it permits people to kill children in the light of day — even to advertise for paying customers to bring the babies in, cash in hand (every Church has a phone book with crystal-clear ads promoting child-killing). Third, it is often covered by insurance programs which do not cover childbirth. Fourth, it is carried out and approved of by the educated cream of our society — the physicians, educators, and lawyers. Fifth, there is an ideological dimension: the feminist movement calls pregnancy the central tool of male domination, and holds that killing her child is an act of liberation for a woman, freeing her to take her rightful place in Western civilization. And finally, to get personal, we — beginning with you and me — have permitted it to continue for years on end.

These realities set the field of combat for the abortion wars. The pro-life movement has attacked on a broad front. Its members seem to be guided by divergent principles even though they could complement each other as parts of a greater whole: political activism, crisis pregnancy centers, care for pregnant and new mothers, public protest, sidewalk counseling, and even bombing (though that has never been organized, and has usually been done by a few very serious-minded people working alone). These various approaches have been going on for sixteen years, but have so far seemed to lack a unifying concept able to galvanize large numbers of people into action more than once a year to fight an evil which delivers painful death 4,500 times a day.

What all of these lack is the physically intolerant intervention of the Cross. It does not matter that physical intervention is not necessarily appropriate to each of these areas, any more than shooting a gun is appropriate to the Army surgeon, Navy chaplain, or even a quartermaster. But without the infantry, the rest of the armed forces will never get the job done. The pro-life movement is like an army. There are more than enough people and related organizations — the hospital units, the equipment, the supply lines. There is even a huge diplomatic corps in constant negotiation with the child-killers, always seeking a political solution. But all these lack the ability to argue from a position of strength. They lack the attack capability to reach through the enemy's defenses and choke it to death, the threat of which will bring on serious discussions. Perhaps the cost of such an effort stretches the war department — it might cost someone his job, rank, or life. But if the enemy is worthy of your engagement, then the only way to get close enough to defeat him is to get close enough for him to defeat you. *The irony of the Cross goes further. The Cross of Christ shows us that the only way to defeat him is to get close enough to lay down your life for him.*

Most assume that the only truly effective intervention is legal intervention — we must make it illegal to have an abortion — only the law can forcibly intervene. But the law is impotent if it is not rooted in the intolerance of a community committed to seeing it enforced. In Canada, long before abortion was made legal, picketers were arrested for picketing an *illegal* abortion clinic, and *a police officer was thrown off the force for refusing to arrest those picketers.* We need more than a change of law; we need a change of heart — hearts no longer afraid to spend and be spent for the kingdom of God. The physical intolerance of the Cross — Rescue — provides that unifying field which can bind the elements of the pro-life movement together, making the Cross the focus of our vision. Only changed hearts will do what it takes to shatter the darkness, because only divinely transformed hearts are willing to die. Evangelism is what is supposed to bring about this heart-change; but if the darkness is not being shattered, then why do we think that our evangelism is converting people to something which changes their hearts?

Were I not serious about the analogy of a body, it would be easy to think that I was conferring some great honor on myself or others when I say that the Rescue sit-ins at the death camp are *central* to the whole pro-life movement, or that the missionaries who commit their lives to this become a *focal point* of what we are trying to do. But the first shall be last. Instead of reason for pride, I see being a focal point in terms of performing the same valuable though ignoble task of a sphincter. There are several of them in the human body. Their function is largely negative. By shutting off passageways, they prevent very unpleasant things from happening. Most of the body's sphincters we never see, and the one we could see we generally do not want to see. But the rest of the body cannot function nearly so well where they do not work properly. We would never hold these limitations against a person disabled in this area. But if a perfectly capable person *intentionally* refuses to control this part of his body, we view him with horror and disgust. So it is in the body of Christ. People are murdering children. We could clamp it off if we were willing to. Are we disabled? Or are we a disgusting spectacle? Only in this sense do I claim that the Missionaries to the Preborn who have taken up their cross have a central, essential role in eliminating the intolerable.

What it Takes

The bottom line to being any part of Christ's body is that if you get involved in one area to escape from suffering in another area, then you will not do that ministry any more good than you did for the ministry you fled. If you are trying to be popular, leave pro-life — no, stop trying to do Christian work of any sort. None of these activities is easy or free of sacrifice. I am not advocating arrest and prison because we have it too soft. I advocate abandoning everything to protect the children because God abandoned everything for us and calls us to go and do likewise if we are to be called His disciples. If you are in any part of the effort to free the world of child-killers, and you are embarrassed by some other part of it — whether they are too wimpy or too hard-nosed for you — you really need to rethink what it is you hope to accomplish.

Every facet of the movement should have as its primary aim the elimination of the killing. There is no necessary conflict between Rescue and any other pro-life activity, except where that other activity (or activist) is formed and motivated by the principle that the choice to kill is permissible. There is a difference between recognizing the reality that the law is on the side of the killer and letting that reality dictate what you *ought* to do. Your goal is to change that reality, not to live with it. Everything you do should be done with an eye to undermining child-killers. Never undermine those who oppose them, regardless of how strident or quiet they may seem to you. Remember how Obadiah and Elijah worked together in God's economy.[2]

The goal of Rescue never was distinct from the goal of any other part of the movement. Rescue rhetoric is not strident; it is standard pro-life terminology with no apologies. We did not invent the idea that the unborn are human; or that killing an innocent human being with premeditation is murder; or that we should protect the innocent. Every part of the movement is strengthened where Rescue is strong. Likewise, Rescues become more effective as every other part of the body is strengthened.

---

[2] I Kings 18. Obadiah was Ahab's right-hand man, but he defied him in order to hide 100 prophets in caves and feed them. Imagine the compromise required to stay afloat as a fearer of God *and* a faithful servant of Ahab and Jezebel! Elijah, on the other hand, put to death 450 priests of Baal. But both men were on the Lord's side, and both are honored for it.

This is why everywhere I have gone in the country to speak for Rescue, I have stressed that as long as God has given us this brief time in the sun to attract people to the cries of the children, we must not hoard those who come to us as if sit-ins were everything. Instead, I have stressed that Rescue communities must pump volunteers into every other part of the battle. Every phase of the process which changes the mind and heart of society must be addressed symbolically, persuasively, and physically. We must match our pro-life arguments with pro-life activities appropriate to the specific end in mind, without abandoning the specific reality which has called us forth: *tiny individual children are being killed today*.

When any other part of the Church supports and advocates Rescue, it is by this connection eliminating the baneful effect of the pro-choice form which it must take so long as it is confined to symbolic or positive intolerance. The comprehensive goal is the same: make killing the unborn impossible by our presence and unthinkable by our teaching and compassion. Then we might have a chance to make it illegal in a way which will last.

In all we do we must show forth the love of God at the core of these efforts in two ways. First we must repent of our failure to be intolerant of child-murder laws. And second, we must not only repent, but become intolerant of the killing in a way that is consistent with each activity, yet modeled after the example of the Cross of the One who was physically intolerant of our sin against Him. He calls us to be similarly intolerant of sin — we die for those whom we oppose, because our goal is their conversion — their transformation.

Chapter 10

THE CROSS
AND THE POLITICS OF RESCUE

We Shall Be Like Him

Winston Churchill had a way of stopping his critics dead in their tracks. We hear that one evening at a formal gathering, one of the matrons of English society became horrified at his drunken state. With the war in full swing, she felt it her patriotic duty to confront him.

"Sir," she said, "you are drunk."

"Madam," he replied, "you are quite ugly."

She gasped at his rude rejoinder, but pressed ahead. "I said you are drunk."

"Yes ma'am," he replied. "And I said you are ugly."

"I do not have to stand here and bandy words with a drunk!" she declared with some heat.

"Madam, permit me to remind you," Churchill calmly replied, "tomorrow I shall be quite sober."

There is a difference between that which can be changed and that which cannot. God's people as presented throughout the Scriptures are always capable of change. In fact, they are destined for change — that is our hope of Glory, that we shall be like Him — and in this change God will change the whole earth. So we take hope, because the Church, like Churchill, is drunk but will be revived. She's not terminally ugly like her critics. This fact should give us, of all people, the hope that changed individuals exert the influence and vision which create changed societies — not perfect, but like us, progressively sanctifying.

The only hope drunkenness offers is that sobriety can return and a sound mind be established before all is lost — a small but very real hope. To that end, it is worth looking briefly at some of the intoxicating doctrines of American Christianity which have led to our current blurred vision and dulled sense of judgment. We will gain perspective on Operation Rescue's shortcomings if we can see how in rising out of the doctrinal stupor of American Christianity, Operation Rescue still inherited many of the built-in problems of a recovering drunk, even while calling us beyond in its vision and action. Rather than standing back in criticism, we should praise God that men and women had the vision to take the steps they did. When walking out of a cesspool, the first steps are often as messy as where we were standing. Still, we do not scorn those steps. We applaud because they lead in the right direction. The politics of Rescue are an example of this.

Lost in the Fog

The discussion of the following doctrines is not to argue for or against any of them, though I have my definite opinions as I am sure you do. Instead of arguing about them, step back for a moment. Whether or not you think them sound doctrines in the first place, look at how they have caused many who hold them to stagger drunkenly in the day of adversity by applying them improperly to their lives. I have chosen them because each doctrine is undeniably an important feature of significant segments of the Church in America today — whether Roman Catholic, Protestant, or Eastern Orthodox — and each misapplication cripples our ministry to a dying, violent world.

1) *The doctrine of the Second Coming.* Regardless of where you come down on this matter — dispensational, pre-, a-, post-, or pan-millennial, pre-, mid-, or post-tribulation — if your views on the appearing of our Lord lead you to ignore the weightier matters of the Law, like justice and mercy, you are in serious trouble. For us, as for the people Amos spoke to, the day of the LORD — the Rapture, or the appearing of the LORD — will be a day of darkness and not light. Hear what he had to say in the fifth chapter of his prophecy to those who were awaiting the appearing of their Lord every bit as much as we await His return. Like us they thought that that meant they could ignore the helpless, the fatherless, and the poor who were oppressed:

> ... You who turn justice into bitterness and cast righteousness to the ground ... you hate the one who reproves in court and despise him who tells the truth. You trample on the poor ... you oppress the righteous and take bribes and you deprive the poor of justice in the courts.... Seek good and not evil that you may live, and

> then the Lord GOD Almighty will be with you, just as you say He is.... *Woe to you who long for the day of the LORD! Why do you long for the day of the LORD? That day will be darkness, not light....* I hate, I despise your religious feasts; I cannot stand your solemn assemblies ... away with the noise of your songs! ... But let justice roll on like a river, righteousness like a never failing stream.... Therefore I will send you into exile.

Because the Church has drunk to excess in its anxious wait for His coming, it has become slobberingly useless to God in His plan to transform all creation.

2) *The Doctrine of God's Sovereign Providence — Election or Predestination.* Though not a popular doctrine today, it historically shaped much of what is good in the form of government we enjoy today. It is also held by many significant leaders in the Church and believed by many in one form or another. But, whatever version of this doctrine you hold, if it leads you to be presumptive of your salvation — thinking you are free to sin because of your eternal security — you are becoming drunk. Or if it leads you to turn your back on the world — which Christ has promised to transform — because "they are not elect," then you have drunk yourself into a stupor in the day of adversity.

3) *The Doctrine of Free Choice.* Today, this is a far more popular doctrine in the Church, since it seems to solve all the problems of evil, and of how God can judge righteously. But it also creates some interesting forms of intoxication. Many who drink deep begin to make man's sovereign choice so fundamental that they end up puking into the same gutter as the predestinarians. They say, "Our only task is to present options and choices, and let the individual's will do the rest." They will no more interfere with a killer's free choice in order to protect his victim than the Calvinist above would save a baby by interfering with a murderer's predetermined will. Thus, they are no more good to a drowning man than a good sermon preached on the bank of the river where he is going down. A society and culture left grasping after words without decisive intervening action of suffering service by God's people on their behalf will be equally lost. How quickly "free choice" becomes "pro-choice!"

4) *The Doctrine that The Task of the Church is Spiritual.*
Who would deny that our task is spiritual? But who defines
what is spiritual for us: Jesus, or Plato? Too often the sincere
desire to be truly spiritual is mixed with the heavy aromatic
liqueur of platonic idealism and eastern mysticism. When this
happens, we find sincere pastors declaring that the spirituality of
the Church prevents her from involvement in the material affairs
of life — healing the sick, feeding the hungry, clothing the
naked, establishing justice, protecting the fatherless, or saving a
life. We find sincere Christians teaching that the laws of the
land are higher than the law of God. Only theological alcoholism
can explain this slovenly lack of resistance to mystical liqueurs.

Together we could list several other doctrinal brews, but the
common point of intoxication is clear — we misuse them to dull
the distinction between our comfortable kingdom agendas and
God's kingdom. We reinterpret each to justify why we can
abandon our Lord's Great Commission to us in Matthew 28:19ff,
"Make disciples of all nations, . . . teaching them to observe
everything I have commanded you; and lo I am with you
always. . . ." Misused this way, they blur the responsibility He
gave us to join Him in His suffering and be made conformable
to His death if that is what it takes to rescue a lost and dying
world. They prevent us from becoming a Romans 8 Christian
whom all creation is groaning to see revealed — we remain the
sort of Christians who will change the world if we can just sober
up.[1] They cause us to forget that the blood of the martyrs is the
most powerful witness the Church can bear to the Truth.

Regardless of where Christians come out in their doctrinal
disputes, we agree to let the world around us go to hell in a
handbasket if only *our* interests would be protected. That
comforting refrain rings through all our competing doctrines:
"Your neighbor in all his created likeness and image of God,

---

[1] There is a coarse street term for "exceedingly drunk" which is commonly
used by my jailhouse congregations. It fits here. However, I will spare
your sensibilities even though Malachi used it of priests and people who
thought that God had to accept just any level of devotion and obedience —
whether in the matter of their tithes or their lives — because they were
"His specially chosen people." Malachi 2:3 says, "I will smear on your
faces the dung of your sacrifices."

body and soul, is not your concern. Your only concern is to minister to that part of him which will not inconvenience you."

Out of this heady mix of save-your-own-soul-at-any-cost, Operation Rescue joined many other ministries in many other arenas, calling for the Church to awake, arise, sober up, and take up the Cross on which Christ died for the whole world — the spiritual and the physical, not just half a world. Therefore it should not be surprising if in Operation Rescue's answer to child-killing there were many areas where we built inconsistencies into our call to rescue. We were dealing with several generations of Christianity not strongly predisposed to break out of the comfort zone and join our Lord outside the camp, and we ourselves were new and untried in our attempts to stand with Jesus Christ at all cost.

Rescue, especially large Rescues, have real political impact. But in a Church besotted by the easy way out, the political promise of Rescue is like the promise of whiskey to a wino. Yes, we might seize political power, but how would we wield it? You cannot seize just enough power to change a few laws. It is all or nothing. We need to seize more than just political power, we need to grow in the integrity to wield it wisely — we need the moral authority which only taking up the Cross can give us. And so we come to the second major problem which beset the Rescue Movement — are we rescuing to save babies, or do we rescue to build the political muscle for someone to come to power?

The Baby vs The Movement

No one in their right mind is against doing things which gain us the power to change the law, and certainly no one is against saving a baby. So how could these two things be in conflict? We could go farther and say that massive attempts to save children from murder will have a profound effect on changing the law, and changing the law will save many lives. Why isn't there complete harmony here?

There is harmony here, because the end which changing the law envisions is the same as the end which saving a child envisions. But there is also a conflict of purpose because to achieve that end, saving a baby and nursing a movement can shape very different actions. Both actions are needed, and both can spill over into the other positively, but they are different. Put simply, one is the call to lay down our lives sacrificially for our neighbors — primarily the children — at any cost. The other is to create political or social momentum, building up a power base to achieve political goals. The conflict comes if we try to build a power base and momentum which will only replace an uncircumcised pagan with a circumcised pagan.[2]

It is the problem of the relationship between the prophetic and kingly functions of God's people. Both are vital to any society. The prophetic call is to all-out sacrifice for what is true. The prophetic road to leadership is to be willing to go to jail for the truth and stay there until our integrity and insight (like Joseph's in Egypt) cause us to emerge as rulers. On the other hand, the kingly road prescribes that we build a political power base through wisely picked battles and carefully nurtured public image. A kingly strategy would lead us to stay out of jail as much as possible, remaining free to organize, speak for our troops, and turn the fervor of saving babies into political capital which can get us elected to power in order to pass good laws and to appoint sound judges who will not legislate from the bench.

These two focal points are justified in two different ways. The prophet is justified by standing for the truth in the face of all opposition. Where Rescue is concerned, the prophet will try to save a life whether he is alone or with a thousand people. Pastor Matt Trewhella of Milwaukee put this well when he said, "If we are trying to fight evil in general, we will become disheartened because there is too much of it for any one person to combat. But if we are in front of the abortion clinic to save the life of particular children, then we can sit in jail any length of time, confident that we did all we could to love *that* neighbor as ourselves even though we might have failed to save his life."

The king, on the other hand, justifies his actions by their popular ability to maintain a coalition sufficient to govern. Thus for the kingly Rescuer, it is numbers, media, and public attention

---

[2] My argument here is only against cheap politics — in which the Cross becomes an inexpedient bargaining chip — not against the political process itself which is the art of diverse brothers dwelling together in unity.

which justify the Rescue or jail stay. That is to say, it is the sense of acquiring movement-building power which justifies saving a baby's life by sitting-in at an abortion clinic.

By building both of these ideas into a single organization a highly-charged moral conflict developed in which the kingly motives were viewed as cowardly posturing, and the prophetic as harsh and demotivating. What did we want to do: save a life or create a movement?

You can find much in Scripture and history to illustrate these two approaches to socially entrenched evil. They are as different as Elijah was from David; as different as Sojourner Truth who led the underground railroad was from Wilberforce who led the British political abolition of slavery. They complement each other. But mingled unthinkingly they will lead to strife and suspicion which divide brother from brother. This is very unfortunate since both are appropriate — even for Rescue at an abortion clinic — but when mingled they led to the disillusionment of many on both sides of the debate.

People are instinctively suspicious that the leaders will manipulate their followers' emotions in one area to gain general power far beyond the specific concerns of the particular issue. Rescue leaders can never seem to escape the questions: "Are you taking a costly prophetic stand just so you can use our sacrifice to aggrandize your power? Is it the babies you love, or is it political office? Are you criticizing some politician because you want to inform us, or because he beat you in the last election? Why do you want us to block doors: to save a life, or to grasp power?"

The world is all too familiar with demagogues who gain authority by cynically preaching the divine for earthly profit. Such charlatans make soul-stirring challenges for the faithful to follow them to hell itself, only to retire from the battle when it gets too hot, taking with them the credibility and offerings earned by the success of the ministry as a whole. The followers are left to start again from disillusioned scratch.

This is the danger which an unthinking mix of the kingly and prophetic brings to the credibility of any leader. Because we built it into the foundation of Operation Rescue, we seemed to end up saying, "We will rescue children at any cost . . . except of course the cost of loss of numbers or of our political and social embarrassment." This way of putting the issue turns the legitimate objectives of a kingly use of Rescue into a grasping agenda hidden behind the noble bluff of our concern for the children — of finding the preborn useful to the extent that standing with them gives us political and social prestige, and keeps the donations coming into our pro-life organizations. *This is a false charge. But the world is only taking this cheap shot where we lay ourselves open, and they have been able to do so precisely to the extent that we have an unthinking dual focus confusing the shape of our efforts.* The only real protection from this charge is the personal integrity of those who are calling us to sacrifice for their objectives.

The Politics of the Cross

We had a hasty desire to speed up the process of earning the right to rule. This is an understandable shortcoming, *and it is not limited to Rescuers.* It is part of that heady brew of doctrines which, making us drunk, causes us to hallucinate about a short-cut to glory — an end-sweep around the suffering service required to love your neighbor as yourself. We looked at four of these misapplied doctrines in the beginning of this chapter. But there is a fifth doctrine which can be added to them, to which much of the Church is being converted today. It too, when misapplied, can cause us to stagger, slur our speech, and uncover our nakedness just as the other doctrines do.

5) God has called His Church to be actively involved in social affairs — to be salt and light. A healthy sign of revival is when more and more Christians discover God's command to see the Gospel change all sectors of life in society. But we must watch to be sure that we do not misapply this truth by using it to say, "Why should we wait? Why should we lay down our lives? Why not conquer in victory? Romans 8 tells us that all creation groans, longing for the sons of God to be revealed *now*. Let us step out in faith and claim it." Yes, the earth groans, and yes, we are being revealed, but not as Torquemadas, Cromwells, or Pattons who rule with a sword, but as representatives and witnesses of the Lamb who was slain, who love not our lives unto death. When the impact of the Gospel's social witness is reduced to a mere drive for success, we fall into the same selfish trap as do those who use their doctrines to avoid having to love their neighbors as themselves. The first four doctrines we looked at keep us from transforming creation by making us afraid to engage the world with the truth. This fifth doctrine, when misapplied, keeps us from transforming the world because it motivates us by the lust to conquer the world. We use the battle cry of "Love your neighbor!" to aggrandize political muscle for our various agendas. Once established, our agendas become sacred cows to keep us in power whether they help our neighbor or not. We reason that however bad our administration might be, it is even worse for our neighbor if we let the other side run things; and so we justify our oppression — witness the sad estate of much Christian political thinking and the Civil Rights Movement today. Both of these are manipulated by cynical power brokers who use the legitimate desire for equal justice under law to gain Christian support for turning Washington into the feeding trough of the messianic new Massa — the welfare state. If we do not have what it takes to lay down our lives for our neighbor, then we will talk ourselves into ruling over him "for his benefit" (and our continued power). Without God's integrity, we will become like the kings of the earth. In our own subtle way, we will change the prophetic obligation, "Love your neighbor," into our own version of the profitable lie, "Power to the people." And like those who fell before, we too may embrace the lie, not as cynical charlatans, but as people sincerely desiring to do right.[3]

---

[3] There are those who love imperfect leaders and plans because they give them a noble excuse to justify why they cannot follow or support any effort. "Not prophetic enough!" say some. "You're too involved in building a political power base for me to join you. When you're *really serious* about laying down your life, I'll join you." Or they say, "Not kingly enough! When you show a serious interest in strategies which are not suicidal, but will work and motivate, then we can work with you."

The Cross, however, destroys these effete pseudo-sacrificial, pseudo-intellectual excuses to avoid serving God. It is why in this book you will not find one line of criticism against anything any pro-lifer *does*. This will frustrate almost everyone, since we all have some activity we want to see condemned. I write to spur you to give yourself wholly to Jesus Christ and follow without fear wherever He leads. Build on those who have gone

It is tragic, but not surprising, that when Operation Rescue burst onto the scene many hoped in it as a short-cut to solving not only the problems of legal abortion, but as a vehicle to address a host of other social issues. But when it slumped they bailed out, their hopes of an easy win dashed. While the righteous uprising is vitally necessary to bring political change, it will never finally succeed if it is not grounded on the kind of commitment the Cross calls us to. For Operation Rescue, the years of "failure" after 1989, though lit by a brilliant success such as Wichita in 1991, are vital years of soul-searching and training in which we must mature to the extent that the Church becomes the force for Rescue for which God hung on the Cross to save and consecrate her.

Use this time wisely to set your house in order!

When the goal of Rescue is to rush to rule, it builds in hay, stubble, and straw. God may count us worthy to rule. Or God may only permit us to lay a foundation for our children's children to rule. That is not our affair. Our task is to win back society's power bases through simple excellence in all we do to obey God in every realm of life. Each Christian should find where God is calling him to give his life, and lay it down there. The pattern of laying down our lives for the children in the womb is the same pattern for every godly walk of life.

Had we done this from the beginning of Rescue, there would be no bogus attacks against us for employing Marxist tactics of gaining power by destabilizing society and government. Where government is false, it is inherently unstable. For a Christian to obey the government at the point it is false would be to confirm and increase it in its instability even though it might appear to bring a form of false peace. Only obedience of the Christian to God will establish sound government and ultimately make false government impossible. And this will happen whether that obedience is inside or outside the political system, whether that obedience is rewarded or punished by the government. *There is no hope of God's blessing us with sound government where Christians refuse to obey God first.* This goes

---

before; lay a foundation for those who will follow.

deeper than thumping for a particular program — though the right program and blueprint are vitally important. It goes to the heart of being a Christian; it is the reality of the Christian way of life. There is only one King. To obey any other king at the points where he commands us to disobey our King, is fornication.

Now it is time for you to open your Bible, turn to Ezekiel 23, and read it — all of it, even though this is where God uses the most disgustingly direct sexual language of adultery and fornication in the entire Bible. He is not railing here against false worship. No, He is heartbroken at His people who look to some kingdom of this world, an Egypt, a Chaldea, or an America, for peace, prosperity, and social stability, rather than looking to simple obedience — to the rule of His provident care. What He warned them against in I Samuel 8, is what they have brought to final full fruition in their lust for a king just like the kings of the earth. For this political harlotry He reserves His most obscenely caustic rebuke. God does not care so much about which king has temporal power over His people at the moment, as He cares about which King His people worship and serve.

We must leave it to the world of false men to declare whether they think we have turned the world upside down. It is not for us to make that an item on our agenda. Whether or not God uses you to turn the world upside down is not your affair. Your business is to be faithfully at your Father's work. His work is Rescue — laying down your life, the fruit of all your abilities, for another. It is the way of the Cross for Christian marriage, business, politics, arts, media. You name the power base you want to rebuild — the Cross is the way. It is the way of I Corinthians 13 love. God's program must be matched with His Cross. Those who are fit to serve and die, God finds fit to execute His program, for only they change hearts.

So, do we rescue to save babies? or do we rescue to build the political muscle for someone to come to power? Both and neither. We rescue to imitate Christ in Whose image we are recreated.

Chapter 11

THE CROSS
AND THE RHETORIC OF RESCUE

Can We Measure Up?

As I sat in his plush office, the senior pastor looked me square in the eye and asked, "Just when will I have done enough?" He looked over my head and waved vaguely at an imaginary bulletin board, "We post everything the Bethlehem Crisis Pregnancy Center asks us to post. We announce all marches and rallies. And still people come up to me and tell me that I'm doing nothing. What's going to satisfy you?"

Without stopping to think I said, "I know what you mean! But don't think you have to satisfy me; I'm easy. I let them kill babies every day. It's the people getting killed in the abortion clinics who are the slave-drivers — as long as my neighbors keep on getting killed, there's more I can do and it drives *me* crazy too!"

I was startled. I was really not being smart. I had not come to talk to him about going to jail or about picketing. I just wanted to know where he stood on the abortion issue. I was a brand new pro-lifer and he was a local pastor. This was my first introduction to the peculiar way abortion gets us all worked up — defensive ourselves and making everyone else defensive.

Why do we all feel as though we have not done enough no matter how much we do? I have come to the conclusion that Rescuers did not invent this feeling, it is inherent in the shock of realizing that we have permitted even one legal abortion. How much more should we expect to be weighed down by the 1.5 million legal murders each year!

Of course when you realize the horror, you step forward to do something. But by then it is too late. Once you step forward, whether you are a strategic king, or a die-hard prophet, the children cry out to you daily to take up your cross. Whoever you are, when you say, "I am going to act like abortion is murder," you are painted into a corner: any day you do not save a child's life seems to become a day of failure.

Is it possible for the Rescue movement *itself* to live up to the demands of the Cross which it made so offensive to others? To live up to the rhetoric of Philippians 2 — to actually be rejected in place of those who are daily led to slaughter — seems impossible. And yet, to fail to come to grips with the demands of the Cross will lead to the discouragement and alienation which afflict any movement unable to bear the weight of its own words.

The way we failed to live up to what we said we would do is not the result of the failure of individuals, whether leaders or followers. Rather it is the result of built-in problems which no leader, organization, or technique of Rescue can possibly overcome without transforming our understanding of what it means to live for Jesus Christ. The Church and the Rescue Movement are now in the process of making just this painful transformation, and this chapter examines the last problem: *any call to defend a child is, in the last analysis, a call to stand with him to the extent that we either protect him, or failing that, be rejected with him — who is willing to take this stand?*

This is a simple fact of life. Publicly murdered infants call for more than politics, more than alternatives, more than sermons, more than demonstrations, more than prayer meetings, pamphlets, and books — they do not call for less; they demand all of these things and more. That "more" must be produced or every other part of the body of Christ will lack a focus and coordination point capable of bringing this particular evil to an end. In Wichita's Summer of Mercy Rescues, Keith Tucci, Director of Operation Rescue National, warned eighty local pastors who had just rescued in that city: "As much as we need to get involved in every other part of the battle, if we do not hold the moral high-ground at the gate of the abortion mills, then we will not accomplish these other things. Mark my words: We will accomplish more by accident through Rescue, than we would if we try to focus on anything else. As you shift your focus, whatever you turn to will slip through your fingers."

God has promised to bring this holocaust to an end. He could end it by destroying the civilization which murders its young — churches, mission programs, big budgets, abortion technology and all; or, God could instead bring the holocaust to an end by transforming His people into cross-bearers who follow Him — who lead through laying down their lives. But the blood of the children cries out for judgment, and God will answer.

This then is the crisis faced by those who know the horror of child murder and have stepped forward to rescue some of those children: *all our words come home to roost.*

What Is Your Price?

To understand our difficulty, remember how Churchill silenced another of his critics. It is how we are often silenced.

Another matron of high society was berating Winston Churchill for how he was conducting the war. She gave him no rest until he finally turned to her and asked, "Madam, would you make love to me for a million pounds sterling?" (Today that would be worth fifty or sixty million dollars.)

The lady was shocked at the vulgarity of his question. But wanting to get on with her point, she thought a moment and decided that one million pounds was nothing to turn up her nose at. "Well, for a million, yes . . . But really what has that to do with anything? As I was saying before . . ."

But he cut her off. "Well, madam, how about for 15 shillings? Are you interested?"

"Sir!" she said in great shock, "Just what sort of a woman do you think I am?"

Fixing his eye on her he said, "Madam, what you are has been established. Now the only question is, what is your price?"

Now that is how the Church silences its critics (Rescuers), and how the world silences its critic (the Church) — find where those who call us to live better lives are themselves inconsistent with their own standards. The world is convinced that Christians are not radically different from anyone else. Recent Gallup polls have even confirmed what the world has already experienced in its contact with the American Church: There is no significant difference between the Church and the world. Therefore, the world believes that regardless of his rhetoric, every Christian has his price. So it is natural for judges and policemen to think that they can teach Christians to protect child-killers the way everyone else does, if they can only discover what their price is. Is it lawsuits? Is it high fines and jail? Is it a wife or husband who forces the rescuing half of the marriage to quit because of internal strife? Whatever it is, the world has one conviction, and it is that — just like them — you too can be bought. Whatever Christianity is, they *know* it does not make you a truly new creature. And this is the horror of our complicity with child-killing — even the complicity of the most faithful Rescuer among us — we, though representatives of Jesus Christ, have lost our credibility.

Richard Cowden-Guido, speaking to Rescuers in Valhalla Prison, put a razor edge to the challenge which the world gives Christians. He said that every time they arrest us, each day they hold us in jail, and each day the Church permits it, is a hideous evil, not because of what they do to us, but because our government, by holding us, and our churches by permitting it, say that each unborn child has no value. To enforce that lie they tell us that each child is so worthless that even non-violent attempts to protect him are wrong, illegal, and will be punished. By honoring God's command to love our neighbor more than we honor their "No Trespass" law, we did not join them in their charade that these children are no more worth our suffering to protect than the human waste matter they join in our sewers is worth protecting. And therefore it is vital to the world that they destroy this witness to a God who really can strengthen us to do all things. The Christian's willingness to suffer, not blindly, but specifically because the people in the womb are as human as we are, exposes this lie as nothing else can.

This is the Great Lie which God calls us to stand against. The abortion culture, through its courts and police, wants to prove all Rescuers hypocrites. "You are happy to grandstand," it says, "happy to force *others* to suffer for the unborn, happy to talk about Jesus and the value of the fetus: but you don't *really* believe it any more than we do, and we will prove it. You have not even been in jail as long as a woman is pregnant, not to say for the 20 and more years of effort it demands after birth. Now that your little stunts haven't worked, now that you are learning what it means to suffer for these children — or for truth, or the will of God, or all your fine sounding talk — you will discover that you agree with us after all, that these kids, fetuses actually (and we hope you'll be honest enough to use that word when you get out of court or jail) these fetuses are certainly not worth suffering for. You will find that you cannot help but agree with the fundamental premise of our abortion culture, which is, *'There can never be any difference between the hungers of the flesh, and the will of God.'* You watch, we will show you that in reality, you are on our side, despite what you say. Just look at yourself: you will stop rescuing in order to surround yourself with the same comforts of the flesh we surround ourselves with. You call it God's will that your fleshly comforts — or Rescue organizations, or churches — be preserved *even if it means permitting these little ones to die today.* And that is what we say about abortion and preserving the opportunity of the woman to surround herself with comforts equal to yours, *even if it means her child must die today."*

The more deeply anyone stands against this lie, the more he will realize how entrenched the American Way is in his own faith; the more he will realize his need to repent and stop judging others; the more he will realize that this calls for daily sacrifice; the more he will realize how low his price is. To wake up from the American dream and serve God daily in any arena requires more than an impulse to activism or altruism. It will cost you your whole life. And that is why, when we launched Operation Rescue, we launched it by calling for profound commitment, even though at the time the work was exciting and the risks were minimal. Such great-sounding words as "Life, Fortune, and Sacred Honor" seemed grandiose, like children playing dress-up in their parents clothes; indeed, that is what we were. Those still rescuing today see less and less excitement, and more of what it will cost. But that is not the reason so few rescue. To understand the deeper reason requires a look at the contradiction we created in our call to rescue — a contradiction which in the end made it seem hopeless to many Rescuers, even as it always seemed overblown to many nonrescuers.

A Center Which Will Hold

The pro-life movement needed to focus those who would be consistent with its description of child-murder, and so that movement gave birth to Operation Rescue. In the same way, the

Rescue Movement had to produce those who would lay aside the things of this life to fulfill daily God's call to protect the children. Without such a center, the rest of the body of Christ — including those whose primary calling is not to pro-life ministry of any sort — would have no way to focus their particular gifts and callings to bring this holocaust to an end.[1]

We faced a contradiction at the heart of our movement: we called for ultimate sacrifice — for that is what the children, Scripture, and the raw facts of abortion call us to — but we only organized safe Rescues which would fit the schedule of the Christian not called to devote his full life to this. This might work on the national level — it is a big country and there are many places to hold low-cost Rescue events — but local leaders soon realized they had no place to hide if they wanted to do it again and again. They either take up a martyr's crown and be crushed by the system, or they retreat and be crushed by their own rhetoric. Most Christians had no objection to saving a baby, but realized intuitively the cost, and so stayed away. But to whom could those who took a stand turn?

What could we do? The rhetoric was sound: they really *are* killing babies; we *can* stop it, or at least stop cooperating with it; God really *does* command us to love our neighbor, and do unto him not only as we would have him do unto us, but as we would do unto Christ Himself. *But how can the Christian not called to pro-life martyrdom have a part in this ministry?* It is necessary that we all be involved. But how? This dilemma trapped more than one leader and crushed him. The call of a sweeping movement minimized personal risk. But the preborn gave us no room to back down should the "movement" disintegrate. The cold fact is that very few leaders, or followers, thought they would actually be left to stand alone behind their words. And most pro-lifers (doubting that the movement would last) refrained from standing up in the first place.

This is not the first time the Church has had to deal with an issue so great that it seemed to eclipse all other issues, calling

---

[1] From here until the end of the book, whenever you read "focal point," rather than thinking such a role to be vainglorious, remember the humiliating analogy of the body on page 120.

into question even our faith itself, and yet so small that it is easy to close our eyes and walk around it as if it did not exist. How can the Church maintain its integrity as a full body of ministry to the world, and yet bring its entire strength to bear on the particular needs of the day?

Historically, to answer this question the Church has produced a core of people to focus the effort each day. It then surrounded that core with spiritual and financial support, and finally, reinforced it with the periodic efforts of the other parts of the body of Christ lending a personal hand from time to time as their primary calling permitted. This is the missionary model.

Rescuing children from murderers need not be different. But when the part-time Rescuer had no center to hold his vision on target — no day-to-day focusing in the lives of full-time Rescuers — a sense of futility set in, and we drifted. Our call to change the world became drum-beating for a particular activist/political agenda — we lost our prophetic edge. As more than one national pro-life leader has told me, "You might as well have turned to politics in the first place and not wasted everybody's time."

This lack of a center is not Rescue's peculiar problem. It cripples the entire pro-life movement so much that most Christians called to other parts of the body of Christ see no meaningful way to become involved in *any* pro-life activity. This is *not* because there are no ways to be involved. Instead, because these things lack a center which is consistent with the nature of legalized child-killing, these actions though good seem futile. And they will always seem futile until we produce a center, a focal point, which will galvanize each person to do what he can with a sense that we are going somewhere — that his small effort isn't just an arrow shot off into the blue. Until then, all pro-life strategies (including Rescue) will sound like one activist agenda among thousands of others in a hundred arenas — poverty, public education, national debt, the drug crisis, souls going to hell. The harried Christian simply asks pro-lifers, "When you have a meaningful solution, call us. I am not called to sign petitions, do a Rescue, picket a clinic, or work in a Crisis Pregnancy Center."

Christians who say this are not condemning pro-life work,

nor are they cowards and compromisers. They are simply people who will never devote their full time to child protection because God *has* called them to other arenas. They fear losing themselves in the endless stream of "more pro-life things you can do." It just is not their calling. And so they stay away with a vague sense of unease and guilt.

The Church needs to impart to each person the vision of his part in driving public child-killing away today and keeping it away forever. It is the spiritual counterpart of stoning. Everyone has something they can do, like a stone which fits their hand and only they can throw. Until there is a focused target, people will feel it a waste of time to throw their stone. But they will gladly throw if they believe that it will go toward blotting out this wickedness in their day. Operation Rescue was another step toward bringing this vision into focus, clamping off the jugular of the child-killers and their supporting culture — a step of selfless compassion. It is worth reviewing in detail how we were able to take this step, how we broke ourselves, and how we can move forward.

"Our Lives, Our Fortunes, and Our Sacred Honor"

These words launched the Rescue Movement in May of 1988. It is the title of the sermon Randy Terry preached Sunday night, before rising at 5:00 Monday morning to lead a thousand people into the heart of Manhattan to close down an abortion clinic for the day — the first of four we shut down that week. As these sermons and letters show, the rhetoric of Operation Rescue left no room to hide. The call to die to ourselves became clearer with each stage of our development.

1987 - 1988 — The Leaders Led in Israel and the People Followed. From the song and victory of Deborah, Operation Rescue envisioned God's people led by their pastors going out in simple obedience, and before the world knew there was opposition, we would expose the horror of abortion, making it a thing of the past — an unthinkable horror even to the media. We did not intended to replace the Church, but to spur the Church to take on its historic task. When the Church would not, we had no *Plan B* to fall back on, and still lack such a plan.

May 1988 — We commit our Lives, Fortune, and Sacred

Honor. We must be willing to sacrifice and pledge support to each other to the death. Knowing the fear of stepping out in a venture as bold as this, we said, "Courage is not the absence of fear, it is doing what is right in spite of our fears."

July - October 1988 — Goliath must Fall. Atlanta's defense of child-killing became symbolic of the entire nation's complicity in murder. While 1,200 Christians were arrested and held in jail over these three months, we declared, "A line is drawn in the sand; Atlanta will be the pattern which the nation will follow. Either we make it safe for children here, or every city knows that we can be bought if they just make the price high enough. Therefore, Goliath must fall!" But Goliath did not fall. In fact, Goliath has yet to fall anywhere.

January 1989 — Jabesh-Gilead: No Covenant with the Enemy. The men of Jabesh Gilead were willing to make a covenant in which they would gouge out their right eye in exchange for protection from the Philistines. This was the message in our return to New York: to defy the $50,000 federal injunction of Judge Ward. It was winner take all, no half-way win, no covenant with the abortion culture: "We must run to the roar, face the greatest threat, or they will know our price. Better to die than to compromise and gouge out our eye."

August - September 1989 — The Lessons from Jeremiah. The terrible crisis of innocent blood facing this country and the inevitable coming judgment requires people willing to sacrifice everything today, and if necessary to rescue where we might be kept in jail indefinitely. "We must be willing to sacrifice to win the war; all we hold dear is at stake."

October 10, 1989 — The October Letter from Atlanta's Jail. Its message so completely brought Operation Rescue to its rational conclusion, that our call to stand is worth quoting at some length: "Winning the war for America's soul will not come easily, cheaply, nor quickly . . . we're going to have to suffer. Some of us may get lengthy jail sentences . . . lose our jobs . . . 'respectable' ministries . . . or homes. But if we are willing to pay this price, I believe we can rescue this enslaved . . . dying nation. I think it's worth it. Do you? [Our sacrifices will] teach our children that there are things worth fighting and dying for. We will leave them a heritage of commitment to the Lord Jesus Christ and His word. They will learn what is important in this life and what is not, what is temporal and what is eternal . . . . If we can endure the hardships God is calling us to, rather than run from them, I believe this movement will grow. If we don't, we may die. As a movement we are at a critical time . . . . Those committed to child-killing have fully blossomed. Will we fully blossom in our holy call to lay down our lives for the children? God help us to do so."[2] The D.C. Project a month later echoed that call to 2,500 Rescuers from around the country: "Now is the time to stand in Atlanta."

October - Thanksgiving 1989 — Go to the Wall or Bail Out Now. The memos to the leadership group planning a return to Atlanta envisioned national Rescue leaders making an ultimate commitment commensurate with the call. Lines such as, "This battle is not going to be won quickly; expect to be here into the summer or fall of 1990," and, "Tell everyone in leadership that they could be looking at three to eight years of jail for felony charges so they should bail out now if they don't have the heart for it." Or, "I don't want our organization to do what it takes to survive, only to have God destroy our country a few years later." These were commonplace in our letters as we planned the second siege of Atlanta. The plan was simple. Because Atlanta was well known as *the* city committed to protecting child-killing, we would make it *the* focal point of the Church's resistance to child-killing. There would be no retreat route. We would call those committed to the end and support them with a national focus over years, if that is what it took. Our goal was not to humble the city, but to do that thing which would bring revival — remain faithful. It was important that churches locally and nationally realize that this focus in Atlanta was not a come-and-go event. They could count on us to stand behind our word regardless of the consequences to us and our organization. We

---

[2] This letter is a powerful summation of all that Operation Rescue stood for. It is worth reading the rest of it to see how it envisioned the way complete daily intolerance of child killing would enhance and focus every other effort to bring it to an end. This letter is the nascent call for the Missionaries to the Preborn, and can be found in *Appendix I* on page 167.

were finally facing for the first time on a national level the normal risk of *any* local organization — they cannot flee from city to city with fresh rhetoric for new hearers. All local leaders *must* stand behind their words and now we were going to join them in their commitment.

Thanksgiving 1989 - January 1990 As the realization set in that a return to Atlanta was not going to produce a quick all-out climactic battle, the question arose as to whether or not it was worth trying at all in a city which showed no signs of life. The discussion in December and January on how to proceed did not involve disagreement over the facts of the national situation. It was obvious that groups were beginning to turn in on themselves as they began to experience decline and exhaustion. Rescue had become "old news" for the media. Groups were turf conscious and skeptical of how expending energy out of town would help their own efforts. For every local and national leader, the threat of the martyr's crown loomed with no hero status to make it seem glorious. A short battle could not muster the necessary intensity, given the condition of the troops. But here were the questions: would a long, patient battle capture the imagination of the Church, grow, and turn the tide? Is it right to lay plans which depend wholly on revival, or should we target something more achievable, like breaking the city's will to arrest and prosecute? What would save the Rescue Movement? The idea that it was time to develop a core of people who would rescue at any cost — that Atlanta would prove our commitment to the Word of God and to the children — seemed hopelessly discouraging to some. Therefore, any who continued this effort in Atlanta could not be associated in any way with the name or concept of Operation Rescue, which was officially shaking the dust from its feet against that city. Any national Rescue leader who remained there would be treated as a rebel.

You can see the dilemma. Our rhetoric left us no place to hide. We had said, "The Church will stand with the children of this city at any cost!" But after the excitement passes what will you do if no one is left standing with you?

There was no place to dodge. We were frustrated. We knew how brave we would be if we could only find enough people to be brave with us. But brave alone? That seemed foolhardy. We had brought the movement to the brink of its rhetoric and realized that we did not have what it took to take the ridge. We discovered that too many of the 50,000 Christians who had been arrested over the prior two years had not been primarily rescuing children at all; we were rescuing ourselves from a profound sense of guilt.

We finally realized what the daily effort to physically shut down a death camp would be, and it overwhelmed us. Who will overcome the punishment barrier until they imprison us, kill us, or leave us alone to act like Christ? Who can be a Christian neighbor to the child? For this is what we said we would be.

If The Cross Leaves No Escape Routes . . .

Our battle cries make clear the dilemma of all Rescue leaders: we had left no escape clauses. This crushed more than one person who signed up to be part of a movement, not to be a voice crying in the wilderness. The legal authorities in some cities like Charlotte, North Carolina, said, "Do what you want," and would hardly prosecute. Others like Atlanta, Los Angeles, and Denver said, "We will crush you." Rescue groups ran the spectrum from "Category Zero"[3] to walking when arrested instead of going limp; from traditional Catholic to wild Pentecostal. Rescue leaders ran from golden-tongued charisma to cold fish; but the overall trend was the same. With few exceptions every group had dwindled, and the promise of the great groundswell had died.

To find a solution, or pin the blame, some people look to leaders, others to methods of Rescue and recruiting, others to philosophical, spiritual, or theological purity. But I am convinced that neither blame nor solutions lie in these areas. It

---

[3] *Category Zero* philosophy is direct and powerful: "We have abortion because all those who believe it wrong are nevertheless willing to cooperate with child murder in order to get on with their lives." Category Zero refuses to recognize the right of courts or jails to hold Christians for saving a life, so they refuse to make "deals" in order to get the legal system to release them, because such deals are only possible because the Rescuer is *born*: the children cannot pay money to protect themselves, so they pay no fines or bail to protect themselves; the children are nameless, so these Rescuers call themselves "Baby Doe," refusing to even give fingerprints — "We will not get on with our lives until the child can get on with his."

is much simpler. Everything necessary has already been said — a good bit of it was said 4,000 years ago. We just need enough foolish people to do the foolish things we claimed God told us to do. The day of the rally is over; the day of doing what we rallied to do has arrived. Don't expect the applause to continue when you actually answer Satan's challenge to God.

We said we would take up a cross, and follow our Lord across the street; and in the end, we will. The world, and even some Church leaders, pray that we do not have what it takes — that in the end we will agree with them that the children are not worth anyone laying down his life every day. As long as there is not the daily sacrifice, they can stand back and say, "What can anybody *really* do about abortion? At least we aren't hypocritical guilt-mongers like those demonstrators, they are so harsh." Within the Rescue movement we argue back and forth about how to woo our critics.

But what solution would you suggest? **Given:** *not everyone will drop everything to rescue daily.* **Given:** *dropping everything to protecting these children daily is what the situation demands. How can the public murder of children call for less than our whole life?* **Dilemma:** *If we tone down our description of the crisis and tone down our call to sacrifice, we are dishonest to our hearers; yet to be honest would leave only a few fanatics in jail.*

Think about it: We all want a national call — a Rescue or a national leader, who turns the tide. But until our hearts change, that call will be impossible. Let me put it starkly: What call can you give to take a stand for the children? If the demands of standing are so small that no one's life is seriously disrupted, lots of people come, but the result will be correspondingly insignificant — abortion goes on as usual the next day, largely unfazed. If you don't keep growing, people feel that it was all a lot of shouting for nothing. On the other hand, if you call for a level of commitment which will actually dent the abortion industry, it will result in penalties so tough that everyone will decline to fight except the people who can take the pain — and not enough of them show up to dent the industry anyway because no one stands behind them; the large crowds seem to melt away. Everyone knows we are at a crossroads, but from

where to where? Is it time to just quit or turn to politics? Or is
it time to rejoice that the child-killers are finally taking us
seriously?

. . . Then How Can We Can Retire Honorably

Jeff White and I stood in a sea of pain watching Assistant
Chief Bob Vernon of the Los Angeles Police personally direct
the systematical brutalization of 1,000 Christians. As the torture
teams — four to a Rescuer — inched closer and closer to us the
fear and resolve grew around us. You could feel it. Jeff
suddenly asked out of the blue, "What would we do if we only
have ten people, some day, to bring out here against 500 cops
and a thousand screaming, biting pro-aborts? Do we rescue?"

Because I had helped launch Operation Rescue, I had often
thought of what I would do when it was over, win, lose, or
draw. There was no question in my mind or hesitation in my
voice as I answered him, "I'm going to find a nice Church;
preach and raise my kids; happy I'd done the best I could. I'm
here to lead a movement, not commit suicide." But as the
decline began later that summer, in 1989, I thought further. At
first I thought it was simply a problem of how we had stated the
case for Rescue. I had helped create a lot of the slogans; surely
I could create new ones which would excuse us from following
through. Everyone knows that Randy can get a bit extreme, go
overboard, and overstate his case? Surely, a more sober eval-
uation of the case for Rescue must show that it is only one activist strategy among others. Then God could call me to a more
balanced life — I could go back to being a good Presbyterian.

So I reviewed what, for two years, we had preached from
the Scriptures. So far did I fail in finding any loopholes, I con-
cluded that we had not even done proper justice to God's requirement to Rescue. Think about it: "He who does not love
his brother whom he has seen, how can he love God whom he
has not seen?"[4] We had not even begun to touch all that the

---

[4] I John 4:20. It is ironic that John, popularly known as that nice apostle
of love, has almost no charity to offer the Christian who fails to love his
neighbor. He goes so far as to make it a hallmark of salvation vs
damnation. Listen: "In this the children of God and the children of the

Scriptures teach and demand in the area of Rescue at a house of legalized murder, quite aside from Rescue as the characteristic of the Christian life. The first three chapters of this book began to form in my heart. I was stuck. Taking up the Cross is not optional. Randy was not overboard in his rhetoric. He was if anything, by God's grace, terribly understated, or no one would have taken the first step. But once we realize where it is all headed, will anyone take the second, or third step?

New and very disturbing thoughts began to grow in me: "Does it really matter whether anyone else in the country *thinks* the children are worth dying for? Even if nobody stands with them, would that change the reality that *they are worth standing with*?" My wife was no help in trying to retire from Rescue. She had come to her conclusions long before I had. "But Anne," I said, "everyone will think we're kooks. What will it mean for *our* children?" Her devastatingly simple answer came straight out of Luke 10:29 and 36: *"They too* are our children."

Jesus went to His Cross alone. Each child is ripped up in his mother's womb alone. At least you might have a family which will stand against this with you. But, even if you are the only one left (and don't for a minute think you are, the rumble is only beginning) who will act like abortion is murder; even if you cannot possibly succeed; does that change where you (or at least somebody) should be? Anne and I could only conclude that God wanted us to persevere. As Anne would often say, "What's the worst thing which could happen? God stops paying our bills, and we have to leave Atlanta and its jails? I can live with that."

But where does that leave the other leaders, not to mention the rank and file? Can they retire with honor? Are they compromisers or quitters if they turn to something else?

If you can understand that the true message of Rescue is that *laying down your life is the obligation; where you do it is a matter of calling,* then you will be free. Those who are not rescuing at abortion clinics must no less be laying down their

---

devil are manifest: whoever does not practice righteousness is not of God, nor is he who does not love his brother." I John 3:10, also vv16-23. We had not scratched the surface of the Scriptures in this business. Is your preborn neighbor *your* brother? (See also footnote 8, on page 75.)

lives; they simply must do it in another arena. This calls for brutal honesty, *"Am I really laying down my life in another arena? Or am I not rescuing at the abortion clinic because I am fleeing the obligation to lay down my life anywhere?"*

This perspective should offer hope, especially to leaders who flog themselves with guilt, or fear the flogging of others:

1) Maybe God did not call everyone who led us to risk being martyrs in the child-killing arena. If not, though they led Rescue groups for a season, they would not lead long-term. They were raised up like King Saul — to break the ice.

2) Even if at first you thought that you would personally pay any price to protect children, there is no shame in being a Jonathan who works to support others whom God has raised up to lay down their lives for the children. You are not eating your words, you are simply finding your proper place in this or some other ministry. But even if you withdraw from Rescue because you simply cannot persevere, let it teach us all how serious God's call is — *how badly we are all out of shape*, unable to meet that or any other call. If we cannot run with men, what shall we do with horses? If it is thus in the greenwood, what of the dry? It is not hypocritical or a failure to urge others on to what we cannot do ourselves. We do this every time we encourage and support someone in another part of the battle, and we should do it for one another in this battle as well. We are only hypocrites when we condemn or ostracize those who press ahead or come behind.

3) God may not have called you to lay down your life for the children daily. Your release from an obligation to rescue at an abortion clinic is not a release from your obligation to rescue in God's kingdom. We do not have the luxury of choosing between a Rescue at an abortion clinic and living in accord with the god of the American Way. You cannot go from the fact, "I am not called to Rescue at an abortion clinic," to the conclusion: "I can return to my old life." The army of the Lord is in the field. You may be able to choose which city you will attack, which part of the army you are in, or to take time to heal your wounds because the battle overcame you. But you cannot leave the battle to eat grapes with David and Bathsheba in Jerusalem.

Chapter 12

THE CROSS
AND THE RELEASE TO RESCUE

The Body of Christ

The day will come when the reality of aborted children burns so deeply into the heart of the Church that tens of thousands will pour out daily into the streets to bring it to an end, providing real alternatives in every Church and every home. And this will be one of the signs that the revival everyone likes to talk about and pray for is upon us. But until then, what will bridge the gap, move hearts, and make that outpouring possible? We need to take the next step. We need a bridge. But what could it be?

It will be Christians taking a step as far beyond Operation Rescue, as Operation Rescue was a step beyond the traditional pro-life movement — a step closer to living Christianity, living faith. As Christians take this step, they will open a way for all other parts of the body to coordinate their efforts to bring the holocaust to an end. Revival — every part of the body of Christ working together to stand for righteousness in every arena regardless of the cost — will be followed by a massive conversion of our land to a faith in more than mere personal peace and prosperity. Without true revival, there is precious little left to which the world can be converted.

Standing against abortion is a key indicator of revival, but not because we think *our* activist agenda is the most important. It is the key because if we will not stand against those next door who rip arms and legs off of little children, God will not give us the strength to stand anywhere. Instead, there will be no revival. He will harden our hearts to further fit us for destruction.[1]

There will be no secular solutions to abortion. This is because abortion is itself the best secular solution to the problem

---

[1] Isaiah 6:9-13; Matthew 13:13-15; Mark 4:10-12; Luke 8:10; John 12:38-41; Acts 28:26-28.

of unwanted pregnancy. It is a solution which makes the whole secular structure of values possible. Removing abortion leaves the secular world with no way to implement its new faith in Man. Legalized abortion like secular humanism — men made gods — is profoundly religious. It will only be replaced by a religion of equal or greater profundity and power. The Cross is the only answer which has the depth and power to overcome this world. It remains to be seen which religion American Christianity will represent. James 4:4 makes this same point far more harshly than any Rescuer: "You adulterous people! Don't you know that friendship with the world is hatred toward God? Anyone who chooses to be a friend of the world becomes an enemy of God."

Therefore, the only solution to abortion, or any other evil which destroys the very fabric of any possible civilization, is to live according to the tenets of the faith once for all revealed, and do so regardless of personal consequences — regardless of the law. For everyone to do so? Yes. But not everyone will. Do we just excommunicate them (before they can excommunicate us)? No. We raise up in the body of Christ the part which will pay the price, so that the rest of the body, through backing up its member, has an instrument which can do the job, and an example which in time it can follow. The missionary to the pre-born is as useless cut off from the body as a hand severed at the wrist. And without that hand, the body has nothing with which to reach through the iron curtain to take hold of the jugular of the child-killing industry.

Missionaries to the Preborn

What if we recast the whole abortion question and ask, "Where is the largest group of people in America who will never be reached by the Gospel?" We would have to answer, "In the wombs of mothers on their way to the abortion clinic." For the Church, the next question must be, *"Are they not worthy to have missionaries sent to them? Not to their mothers, their congressmen, the aborting doctors nor clinic staff, **but to the children themselves** — are they not worthy?*

How can the 4,500 unreached people who are scheduled for murder today be reached by the Gospel? In the same way the

Church reaches all unreached people — by sending missionaries into the harvest. The unique call of the Church is to minister the Gospel to everyone for whom Christ died, regardless of the cost, or where they live — Borneo, France, inner-city, or womb.

There are 400 different mission groups in America, and yet until now none of them has chosen to reach this group of people with the Gospel. Each day 4,500 of their number are slaughtered with no chance to hear and see what the Gospel means in the lives of God's people. These are the children whose mothers reject crisis pregnancy centers, walk past the picketers, are unmoved by sidewalk counselors, and who are brought into abortion death chambers — these are the children God calls us to reach out to and protect at any cost to ourselves.

There is no way to reach these needy children without crossing to the other side of the iron curtain of American law which has descended protectively around the abortion industry. The Church's missionaries to the preborn reach through that curtain to rescue those children from certain death. The Church has long supported ministries and missions which reach behind the various iron curtains in our world. In these other iron curtain ministries, we do not limit our outreach to word only, otherwise radio ministries would fulfill God's commission. In addition, we know that we must send people where it is illegal for them to go, with a message it is illegal to preach, doing things (such as Bible and clothing distribution) which it is illegal to do — ministries such as Eastern European Missions and Operation Mobilization. The Christian missions to Korea and Japan were begun when the missionary was forbidden by law even to enter the country — on penalty of death. But they came anyway, and Christians were martyred, by the thousands.[2]

---

[2] This century has seen more Christians murdered by their government than all other centuries put together. It has been illegal in some countries even to state your identification with Jesus Christ. But in others, like America, though it is legal to *profess* your identification with Christ, it has become illegal to *act* as if you belong to Christ. We must get beyond the romantic attachment we have to America and realize what Hosea's wife, Gomer, refused to realize: that it is God, not America, Who has blessed us, and that only God can continue to bless us, whether the American state wants to be a part of that blessing or not. You must read *By Their Blood*, by James and Marti Hefly, 1988, Baker Books.

Today in America it is illegal to protect unborn people. When it is illegal to save a child from murder, it is illegal to be a Christian. The law has made it illegal to act like Him who said, "Whoever receives one little child like this in My name receives Me."[3]

The weapons of our warfare are no different from the weapons of warfare in any Christian ministry which governments have made illegal. God's weapon is His people's willingness to put themselves in the line of fire intended for those to whom they minister, joining them regardless of personal cost. The weapon and power source of all spiritual warfare is the Cross: physically intervene, in a way which is harmless, in a way that brings suffering to yourself rather than to the intended victims or their persecutors. In our case, that person is the helpless child, and the cost of standing with him to protect him is beatings by police and pro-abortion thugs, mock trials, imprisonment, and lawsuits which make it impossible to own anything.

What is a Missionary? Someone who believes that God is calling him to lay down his life to reach people for whom Christ died. Missionaries are committed to represent the Church; they are committed to a particular field; they are committed to minister to people who would not normally hear the Gospel; and they commit their whole life.

Then, what is a Missionary to the Preborn? Everything any other missionary is. His unique commitment is to rescue the children in a particular area; whenever he is free of jail; until he is free to rescue every day; until it is as safe to save a baby's life as it is now safe to kill him; until they finally stop the killing. Missionaries to the preborn reestablish the historic reputation of Christians as those who stand for life, whether or not the state has made saving a life legal or illegal.

The Cross, the Church, and the Children

Hearts will change as Christians redefine the issue in Biblical terms. These children in the womb are people in need of Christians who believe the Gospel is Good News for *them*

---

[3] Matthew 18:5.

also. Whether the aborted child is saved or unsaved, the Gospel, to be effective for him, must begin where God began with us — with protecting his life.[4] If you believe that some children who are murdered go to hell, then you must rescue them so as to give them the possibility of hearing the Gospel and seeing it acted out in the Rescue itself. If you believe that the aborted will go to heaven, then you must believe that they are the brethren of our Lord. According to Matthew 25, to reject protecting them is the same as rejecting our Lord Himself. Because there is nothing to indicate that His brethren in the womb are excluded by this verse, Matthew 25:46 teaches us that to fail to protect His brothers is to call into question *our* salvation.

We are finally leaving behind the controversy of Rescue as a strategy — a means of highlighting a social evil by periodically demonstrating our abhorrence of it and the illegitimacy of the laws which protect it. Instead, the Church is raising up those who will express the deepest elements of her faith in simple obedience. As the corporate body of Christ, she will do for the children a small bit of what our Lord did for us — she will, in their place, bear their rejection. She will do this by raising up people who will rescue as often as they are not held in prison. They represent all of us. All Christians are called to bring the Gospel to the gates of hell and bear His reproach as a way of life, not a periodic demonstration of sincere intent. We cannot

---

[4] Genesis 3:7 is one of the most remarkable verses in the Bible: *Life continued after the fall into sin.* How could God let that happen? How and why could He protect our lives, especially when so many of those He protected were going to hell anyway? The Cross. God protects each physical life as a starting point for the Gospel itself. If He did not keep us alive — even as rebels — then He would have had no one to save.

For us, we do not normally have to save someone's life in order to tell him the Good News, but for those whose lives are wrongly threatened, we do what God did — save their lives. And we protect them whether or not they are our brothers in Christ, because He protected us long before we could call Him our elder brother.

It is the transforming work of God the Holy Spirit which enables our effective witness to the providential hand of God the Father, by joining the selfless work of the Cross of God the Son — "That I may know Him and the power of His resurrection and the fellowship of His sufferings, being conformed to His death." Philippians 3:10. "I now rejoice in my sufferings for you, and fill up in my flesh what is lacking in the afflictions of Christ, for the sake of His body, which is the Church." Colossians 1:24.

all do it in every arena in which the Church is called to warfare. Therefore, the missionary — whether he rescues at the abortion clinic, in Borneo, in the business world, or by raising lots of children in the nurture and admonition of the Lord — he becomes the representative of the Church, whose dedication and effectiveness in his particular arena is no more or less great than the dedication of those he represents, for they represent him in other arenas. Around them, the rest of the battle and all the other gifts take on meaning, direction, and depth.

I believe that God has given the Church everything necessary to change the world. The pro-life movement followed the model of political and social action, education, and soup kitchens. Operation Rescue, modeling itself after the camp meeting and the crusade, came a step closer to the Church. In the arena of child-killing, I believe it is time to turn the Church back to its own historical and Biblical roots: Gospel missions.

Released to Rescue

The Christian in all of his life is released by God from sin and death in order to rescue. Throughout the Gospels and Letters, we are commanded to take up the Cross in our daily lives. The sacrifice of the Cross was an act of grossly physical intervention which made possible the spiritual and physical reality of redemption. The spiritual authority of the Church and of individual Christians will always have a physical dimension — *and so do we when we rescue.* For it to be possible for the Cross to be presented to mankind as God's solution to evil, our Lord had to be harmless and submit Himself to those who would destroy us if He did not stand in the gap to be destroyed in our place — *and so we are harmless while keeping others from harm.* He specifically rejected revolution and political activism as lasting solutions, and instead took all violence to Himself in place of His people, because He would settle for nothing less than the heart-changing transformation of the world — *If we would do our small part to win the world, then "ministry" and "leadership" must mean imitating our Lord's self-denial.* Finally, the Cross is the supreme expression of the incarnation, where God emptied Himself and became flesh, ultimately suffering for us outside the camp, becoming sin in our place.

Hebrews 13:12-13 tells us that the call of salvation is this call to join Him there outside the camp. Philippians 2 makes this the pattern of the Christian life — *we must have the mind of Christ and put the business of others (including that of the people in the womb) above our own as He put our lives above His.*

We will not all rescue in the same arena — but we are all called to find how the Cross applies to the arena where God has called us to RESCUE, and lay down our lives for others there. In the arena of children whose mothers will not be turned back by any other means, I do not know of any other approach which incorporates these three aspects of the Cross: physical intervention, harmlessness, and emptying oneself to the status of another by taking on his weaknesses and punishment in the act of protecting him.

If Christians are to continue to rescue children in a particular city or state, sooner or later they must be able to overcome whatever punishment the courts — by permission of the local churches — deal out, and then return to rescue again. *These fines and long jail sentences are nothing more than the world's re-education program for Christians who dare to return to rescue. The missionary will overcome them by making his release from jail a release to rescue again.* The courts want to know what it takes to re-educate us — to make us learn that we cannot protect children here. What is our price?

This problem is not unique to a Rescue from abortion. It is the problem of every mission field of the Church: Satan wants the price so high that no one will dedicate his life in any arena. Because not everyone will go, sending missionaries is how the Church pushes beyond this impasse. For the analogy of the body to work, *someone* must go and the rest of us stand behind him. Regardless of the obstacles faced by the missionary in any field, when he overcomes them, he overcomes them to continue his work of Rescue, not to retire and enjoy the good life. God's people are always released from their trials to rescue.

When we apply this to a Rescue at the abortion clinics, we say that the full-time missionary to the preborn reaches the children in the name of God's people. By supporting him we join him as we can, no longer burdened by a load of rhetoric we cannot bear. We prepare for the day when every heart shall burn to end this murder in our midst.

There has been an ongoing debate within the Church, often splitting us. We argue technique by the hour: technique for baptism, liturgy, evangelism, and missions. In Rescue circles the same sort of argument rages about the best way to rescue. Perhaps the insight of the missionaries — *that we are released from trials and prison in order to rescue* — will help cut through these problems in the Church.

The missionary principle of being *released to rescue* cuts through the Gordian knot of how to do the "perfect" Rescue. The missionary focuses on the heart of where we stand in solidarity with the person in the womb: at the door of the death camp, keeping his killer away. Regardless, then, of how one deals with the system, when he is released — whether from probation or jail — the only question will be, "Has the Christian been re-educated by *this* legal system in *this* town to stand aside and let them kill *these* children? Or will he return to those death camps as soon as it is possible for him to do so, to resume his part in the ministry to the preborn? And if he cannot personally return, will he make it possible for others to represent him?"

For the Church at large we would broaden this principle to say, *that we are released by God from sin and death in order to rescue in His kingdom.* We must not fight over details of technique if that keeps us from doing what we *know* we must do.

What we strive for is to be consistent rather than insist on proper technique. Will we be faithful to do our best? This same principle of *consistency above technique* applies to those who support the missionary. If someone's part in ending child-killing is to amplify the missionary's work by calling courts and judges, prayer, and financial support, then they will do that with a daily zeal, purpose, and a faithfulness against all odds, which match the missionary's.

Finally, for those primarily involved in any other sort of ministry in the body of Christ, this same sacrificial call to faithfulness in their arena will lead them to do all they can to maintain the Church's uncompromising hostility to the world. "Friendship with the world is hatred toward God."

CONCLUSION

THE CROSS BEFORE ME
THE WORLD BEHIND ME

"Let goods and kindred go. This mortal life also. The body they may kill, God's truth abideth still. His Kingdom is forever."

"You won't believe it!" shouted Joe Washburn as he stormed into my house one day last summer. "I've been to three Christian bookstores because I needed the exact quote to that verse in *Faith of our Fathers* which goes something like, 'Our Fathers chained in prisons dark were still in heart and conscience free; and truly blest would be our fate if we like them, should die for Thee.' And I can't find one hymnal that has not deleted the verse! Not one modern hymnal! Check them yourself, you won't believe it!"

I did. I believe him. With this sort of erosion to our foundation, is it any wonder that the issues of this book leave many offended? Not only have we been trained to seek the easy way out, one of the first things we do when we feel guilty is absolve ourselves by finding a shortcoming in the one whose message has made us feel the guilt. And no one has to look far to see how far short I myself fall, when even the most faithful Rescuer is an easy target.

When I try to explain to my children or to God why I don't save babies every day, I feel like someone explaining to his wife that he is only unfaithful once a year. "But honey, you are far more important than this other person. I love you the whole rest of the time." Rebuking the Church, I sound like the man who criticized others for having an affair monthly, only to tell them to be pure the way he was: unfaithful once a year at most.

Making people feel guilty for things even pro-lifers were guilty of was a major hurdle for the pro-life movement. The Rescue movement inherited a double portion of it. Our own words find *us* as guilty as the nonrescuer. As radical and righteous as

159

Rescue sounds at first, we were not even close to being as radical or righteous as our own words demanded we be. *Listen to what we said with our words: "If you call abortion murder, then act like it." Now listen to what we said by our actions: "Even though they murder every day, we only need to 'act like it' with a sit-in three to twelve times a year."*

When we realized this inconsistency, many quit Rescuing altogether. Others just lived with the tension and did the best they could. Others became irrationally bitter, knowing they would have the courage to be consistent with their Christian confession if they could only get enough people to be consistent *with* them. Still others sought to do the impossible, to tone down their Christian convictions so as to be less offensive.

But that center is now forming which will bring our words and our actions together, making each meaningful. The daily commitment to rescue at any cost justifies the occasional mass Rescues as part of a greater whole, even as the mass Rescues legitimate the daily effort to save life. Taken together they show that the missionary Rescue is not isolated fanaticism, nor is the occasional Rescue (or any other part of the pro-life movement) hypocritical.

We have been forced to stop arguing about whose sackcloth is hairier or whose cross is bigger. We are realizing that there is only one matter at hand: "Will *I* repent? Will *I* take up the Cross at all?" If I answer, "Yes," then it is only a question of which arena I am called to die in. It does no good to criticize others for what they do or fail to do. The question for our Lord in Gethsemane was not, "Will Peter go to the Cross with You?" But, "Will You go to the Cross for Peter even though he sleeps through Your dark night of the soul, flees from You, and denies You?" As Rescue missionaries take up the full-time challenge, work in the dark, and leave organization to others, a wholeness can be restored to the movement. Each can do his part with no sense of shame that we are leaving something undone — the body will become an apt analogy again. As the Lord restored Peter after his denial — even though Peter had returned to fishing because his life did not match his rhetoric — our Lord comes to each of us who have failed, in order to restore us.

If Rescue missionaries become obsessed with their own

sense of sacrificial importance, they will accomplish nothing. And if nonrescuers resent Rescuers and limit the Church to solutions which fall short of what her own Christian confession and faith demands, and yet talk as if the body of Christ is doing all it can, then we will have child-killing with us until God removes our lampstand in disgust.

In the past, there were too many people who wanted to make our failures and their inabilities the norm for Rescue and the Church, as if a higher call is inevitably doomed because *I* cannot personally respond to it, or I see that *you* are imperfect in your response to what you preach about. Yet what we are seeing today is a growing sense of restoration, recommitment, and moving ahead. For the Church is to be an overwhelming flood of compassionate, intolerant light rising to destroy child-killing and restore the very foundations of Western civilization. Without this rising flood of light, the missionaries to the preborn are but candles on a glacier.

That light is shining stronger every day. In those cities where the legal system follows each Rescue with weeks or months of jail, these witnesses — these Missionaries to the Preborn — become the opportunity of every Christian to hold the entire legal system accountable each day for the murder it protects. In so doing, they will free the missionary to Rescue every day the doctor is killing, until it is as safe and legal to protect children as it is now safe and legal to kill them. Where there are missionaries, the issue is not, "Will you rescue?" but, "Will you so much as make *one brief phone call a day* to enable others in your city to bring the Gospel to the people who live in the womb?" God is not asking, "Will you go to jail for Me, or die for the little ones." No, the question is now very simple, "Will you even pick up a phone and plead for those who *would* rescue them if only they were out of jail?" We may well be only a telephone call away from judgment.

As God moves in the heart of His Church, daily phone calls will begin to pour into the courts, demanding **"Let My people go, that they may serve Me!"** Courts will be astounded that Christians do not support this system which protects killers. The courts will argue that if they let these Christians go, they will only go "break the law again!" But they will not be dealing with the gullible, state-worshipping, leave-it-to-Beaver Christians of the 1950's who have no answer to give. Instead, they will be dealing on the phone with thousands of Christians like you, who call daily asking, *"Are the Christians out of jail yet? . . . No? . . . Why not? . . . No they didn't break any laws, they saved lives . . . Yes, of course they will go back to the abortion clinics and try to save more lives . . . Yes, the abortion clinics. That's where they kill the babies, so where else would you expect a Christian to go? . . . What? . . . No . . . NO! . . . How can it ever be against the law to save a life? Tell Judge Hill to let the Christians out of jail so they can continue to serve God!"*

The message of the Church is not, "Free us so that we can go back to our pursuit of the American Dream." But, "Free us to go back to the death camps until they are gone. This city, this nation, is too small for Christians and child-killers to live in the same place." We will send this message to the judges daily.

A Milwaukee Missionary illustrated this commitment. On June 29, 1991, the Milwaukee Missionaries to the Preborn hosted a Rescue with YOuth For America, a national organization for young people who have survived the abortion holocaust. After an hour of waiting to get into his death camp, Dr. Seamars, the commandant (operating under his wife's name for fear of public discovery), shouted out in frustration, "This isn't going to make me quit."

Michael Foht replied from the front door, "I've devoted my life to making you quit killing children. Take a good look at me, Dr. Seamars; *I'm fifteen years younger than you!"*

Four months after this encounter, thirty-three year old Doctor Seamars was still killing children, but his youthful brown hair had turned completely white from the daily presence of these Christians dogging his steps with Good News for his victims — and Good News for him, would he only stop to listen. Finally he had met Christians whose dedication to the LORD of Life matched his dedication to the gods of death. They are not nice Christians; they are real Christians.

The next day, week, month, year, decade, will find the same Christians there at the death camp, there in jail, there in court, there on the phones. Growing, always taking another step forward, as more and more realize there is no common ground with child-killing. They will be eyeball to eyeball with every part of our legal system which keeps them from protecting children. And because a few are unflinchingly eyeball to eyeball, they bring the rest of the Church within striking range. There will be no strategic talk of "soft target cities" versus "hard targets." All baby-killers will be seen as God's target, and we will take them out by laying down our lives for them. We will stop running *to* the roar, or *from* the roar. Every child-killer in time will have hordes of Christians dogging his every step, even blocking any steps which take him closer to a killing center.

Missionaries take an attitude toward abortion which forces it to become a "me or you" issue — or rather, a "me *for* you" issue. As they do this, the rest of those against abortion will reflect that same implacable determination to rid the land — not fight abortion, but to rid the land of it. These missionaries will become the cutting edge of the Church's historic intolerance to the murder of the innocent. They will represent the Church as they give the world the four historic options the Church of Jesus Christ has always offered a hostile world whenever it has made it illegal for Christians to act like Christ: 1) flee your perversion, be converted, and act like Christ; 2) leave us alone to live like Christ; 3) put us in jail forever; 4) or kill us — but we will act like Christ!

Will the Church turn because we have finally converted it to activism? No. The Church will turn only when she finds a Biblical way to express the unity of the Body of Christ and His crucified love in her intolerance on behalf of His little ones.

Five Conclusions

1) *No solution to abortion that is not distinctly Christian will be a lasting solution.* This is because abortion itself is one of the costliest solutions to any problem imaginable. In essence, through abortion we permit people to publicly murder the innocent witness to their sin, or we let them murder the child who might cost too much for any of us to love and care for. Any solution which successfully replaces the solution of abortion will of necessity be equally costly. Only the Cross evidenced in the lives of God's people will provide such a solution. All

solutions await revival.

2) *Operation Rescue as a concept and as a movement was headed in the right direction, but still held too many presuppositions of the world — presuppositions held by most Christians themselves — and, like the American Church, lacked foundation in people willing to pay the price of their convictions.* The major worldly presupposition was that suffering to meet the needs of others is optional, and therefore a crusade of idealists seizing earthly power would be an equally effective way to accomplish God's will. It was child's play to turn the energy of protecting children into political or social activism — to trade the legitimate political success brought on by a Rescue Crusade for a political illusion brought on by the thirst for power. Satan continues to offer God's people the kingdoms of this world just as he offered them to Christ. And we still long after earthly power, whether through normal politics within the system or sit-ins outside the system, without stopping to earn the divine character to wield such power wisely. God's counter-offer is a cross and His kingdom founded in heartfelt loving obedience at any cost. Only out of the standards of righteousness and the sacrifice of the Cross can politics become Christian, redemptive, and fruitful. All too easily the world proved that we were not willing to sacrifice to save a life. If they continue to prove this, then they are correct to suspect that our political solutions will be little more than forcing others through law to carry burdens we do not lift a little finger to carry ourselves: we ask the young mother to sacrifice for us either her child through abortion, or her life-style by bearing the unwanted child. The Cross has a more perfect way — love laying down its life for another, whether at the death camp, in jail, or opening up your own home to house the lonely, feed the hungry, clothe the naked, protect the weak, provide for the fatherless, shelter the widow, and defend the orphan.

3) *The nature of legalized abortion in America is such that it presents the Church with a fresh version of a very old problem — today it has once again been made illegal to act like Christ.* When it is illegal to physically protect another human being from murder, it is illegal to act like Christ. Will we act like the world and protect child murder, or will we act like Christ and protect

and provide for these children? I do not believe that we will see an end to child-killing until enough people do for the children what Christ did for us — make it a personal matter of life or death to protect them. We are gathering those people together, one missionary, one supporter, at a time, who can say to the child-killer: "It's you or us, from now till the day either you quit killing or we die." We want to live at least as consistently with our beliefs as the abortionist does, and commit at least as much of our lives to standing with the people in the womb as he commits to standing against them. Through their representatives, the churches in each city will be able to say to Satan at his death camps what the Gospel says to Satan in the world, **"There is no place on earth that is big enough for killers and Christians to live together in peace. The Church will be the Church."**

4) *There will be no lasting solution at law, in alternatives, nor education, until enough people treat the preborn as their human equals.* When we begin to treat them as truly equal to ourselves, we will find that there is a tremendous price to be paid. Only by paying that price will we purchase the necessary respect for the preborn to have their inalienable right to life respected by the rest of the world. In so doing, we will begin to realize how much value our Father puts on His image bearers — enough to cause Him to take on our flesh, take up a cross, and call us to sacrifice with Him outside the gate. When we join Him, in the words of Philippians 3:10-11, "being made conformable to His death," then true change — from the heart — of men and societies can take place, and we will "know the power of His resurrection."

These missionaries will not replace Operation Rescue any more than Operation Rescue could replace the pro-life movement, or the pro-life movement could replace the Church. They represent the first-fruit of the return of the pro-life movement to the Church from whence it came. They are an expression and focusing of God's command to become intolerant of evil by loving and serving God only, and loving our neighbor as ourselves. They are pioneers in a mission field long neglected by the Church, reaching with the Gospel to those who will never hear it in this life if the Church shrinks back. In short, we will effectively deal with abortion only when the Church grows up and starts acting like the Church.

5) *Revival is not when unbelievers come to Christ, but when believers come to Christ.* In the next several years, revived Christians will converge on one city, not to battle that city, not to make a great media splash, but to become a part of the churches there who are rising up in the name of the Lord of the Church to make child-killing impossible by their presence, unthinkable by their teaching and personal example, and finally illegal by default. From that example it will grow. The Church in each city around the country will take courage, because God will begin to move in His people. Understanding of abortion in all of its intolerable horror will spread. God's people will reclaim their heritage. Pastors and congregations will unite to challenge the killers, saying publicly with a voice that unites all sectors of the church which confesses Jesus Christ as its LORD,

> "Go ahead and sue us. We would rather lose all our property than go down in history as the Church which bought its peace and prosperity with the blood of innocent children. We are tired of that blood running through the streets of our cities. We are tired of trying to pretend that we cannot see our own footprints where we have tracked their blood into our businesses and homes. We are made sick by the trail of innocent blood which leads down the aisles of our Churches, fouling the pews where we kneel to worship God — the murder of little ones is not debatable. It will stop. So you may as well come after us, because we are coming after you."

We will show, city by city, that the time has come for the child-killers to leave town and kill somewhere else. This will not be the heroic effort of a few isolated fanatics, but will represent the focused effort of the entire Church as each part of the body coordinates its work around the center of those who refuse to stop protecting children regardless of the cost — refusing to stop, even to organize others. The entire Church will focus clearly on the target, each member throwing the stone God has given him. Thus "shall you blot out the memory of Amalek from under heaven" (Deuteronomy 25), shattering the darkness.

APPENDIX A

LETTERS FROM FULTON COUNTY JAIL

On September 30, 1989, Randy Terry was given a two-year sentence in Fulton County Jail, Atlanta, which was later reduced to one year, of which he would serve 4 months. The first of these letters was sent to about 30,000 people. The second was sent to Atlanta area pastors. In them, he shows his great ability to launch a movement. Perhaps, more than any other document, these letters brought the call of Operation Rescue to its rational conclusion. His October 10 letter was originally the call to return to Rescue in Atlanta and pay any price to protect children there. But it became the catalyzing call for a deeper level of ministry to grow out of Operation Rescue — a ministry which has now grown to become the Missionaries to the Preborn. *This missionary fellowship is springing up in cities across the country.*

In these letters, Randy has outlined with remarkable accuracy not only the need to find those willing to take up their cross in Rescue, but how Christians being faithful to Rescue would invigorate every part of the pro-life movement and Church to take up the Cross sacrificially in whatever they do throughout all society.

* * * * *

October 10, 1989

Greetings in the name of Jesus from the Fulton County Jail,

Please read this letter prayerfully and thoughtfully before the Lord. I want to share with you . . . some burdens I have about the Rescue Movement; where we've come from, where we are, and where we may be going. . . . I am deeply troubled by what I see happening to the Rescue Movement nation wide. In city after city (with a couple of exceptions), the numbers of rescuers are shrinking, and the average number of rescue missions per week is dropping.

Why? Why this downhill trend? **The cost.** People are starting to ask, "Is this worth it? Can I afford to keep rescuing children? Am I willing to risk *this* or *that* in order to stop this holocaust?" I was reading in Exodus today and a couple of verses struck my heart. Exodus 13:17 says: "When Pharaoh let the people go, God did not lead them by way of the land of the Philistines, although it was near; for God said, 'Lest the people repent when they see war, and they return to Egypt.'" When God first delivered them, He didn't want to expose them to heavy fighting, because He knew they might retreat back to Egypt. That made sense (even though eventually they were going to *have to fight* to take the Promised Land).

But then I thought, *"God, how could they go back to Egypt?!"* Egypt, the land of oppression. Egypt, with all its false gods. Egypt the land of royal edicts for Jewish mothers and midwives to kill newborn Jewish boys. Egypt where their children and grandchildren would be condemned to a life of slavery for generations. The truth is

167

simple — *they would rather have the stability of the status quo, even if the status quo were perpetual slavery, oppression and death,* than to have to fight a war; a war where the stakes were high: loss of material goods, injury or even death.

I fear we have become just like them. I'm afraid we aren't willing to pay the price to end child-killing. Now that we've begun to taste war, many of us are "repenting" in the bad sense. We are turning back from the battle. We would rather have the status quo — our current jobs, homes, no long jail sentences, etc., than an "all out war" against child-killing, even though the status quo means millions more dead children, oppression and tyranny for *our* children and grandchildren, and probably the ultimate destruction of our nation.

Let me state it plainly. A lot of us in leadership are losing our nerve, wavering in our courage and determination. A lot of us in the rank and file are losing our nerve, and are retreating from the front lines. We have consciously or subconsciously said that the **cost is too high, forgetting what terrifying horrors await us and our families right around the corner.**

I've read and reread Jeremiah lately, and I encourage you to do the same. I have come away seeing a frightening reality that oppression, tyranny, and destruction are stalking the church and the nation. In a short few years, we may find ourselves hiding in the hills to protect our families, or locked up in huge holding facilities. We may find our churches seized, closed or burnt to the ground; our children being taken by the state, our women violated; terrorism on American soil; a national economic collapse so great that you may have to spend your life's saving for a loaf of bread; drought and famine so severe that people actually degenerate to *cannibalism.*

Do you think it impossible? Do I sound like a half-crazed alarmist? This is exactly what Jeremiah warned them God would do because of child sacrifice and other abominations. We may be *more* wicked than they were. If God didn't spare Israel, *why should He spare us?*

Let me ask you this: In 1959, if someone had stood in an American pulpit and declared, "In 30 years we will have murdered 25 million children in the most barbaric ways imaginable; we will be killing handicapped newborns and unwanted elderly; prayer and Bible reading will be illegal in public schools; homosexuals will be marching in the streets; mayors in prominent cities will declare 'Gay Pride Week'; we will have a terrifying plague known as AIDS; Christian schools and home schools will be harassed by the government; Christianity will be mocked on TV sitcoms; Hollywood will produce a blasphemous movie, 'The Last Temptation . . .'; pornography — the debasing of women and children — will be rampant; children will be kidnapped and murdered in 'snuff' films; we will have government scandals beyond belief; hundreds of thousands of homeless; a cocaine crisis that is threatening the very security of our nation; and school officials in New York State suggesting we teach third graders about condoms and anal sex." *WHO WOULD HAVE BELIEVED IT?!*

Would not such a person been labeled a lunatic?

If America has slid into the very mouth of hell in 30 short years, where will we be 10, 20, or (if we're here) 30 years from now? What living nightmares will our children face? You don't have to be a prophet to see that we are in deep, deep trouble before God.

Brothers and sisters, please hear me. The battle to end child-killing has been joined in earnest. In reality, this is a battle for America's very survival. We will not, we *cannot* survive as a nation if we continue to plummet down this path of violence, murder and moral anarchy.

But winning the war for America's soul will not come easily, cheaply, nor quickly. Child-killing is entrenched in our culture and the death forces will not be dethroned overnight, or without a serious fight. It's going to cost us to reform this country. *We're going to have to suffer.* Some of us may get lengthy jail sentences; we may lose our jobs and be forced to take ones that pay less; we might lose some of our "respectable ministries", our possessions, our homes, or not be able to drive the kind of car we like. In short, we may lose our nice "safe stability". **But, if we are willing to pay this price, I believe we can rescue and restore this enslaved, violent, dying nation.** I think it's worth it — do you?

If we *won't* pay the price, we will most assuredly lose all our "safety, comfort, and possessions" anyway, and with them the future for our children. America will lie in the ash heap of history, testifying against our cowardice and selfishness, with our children and grand-children bearing the full brunt of the brutality and chaos that is coming. **The cost of *not* fighting is too great.** Let me ask you this: would you do anything differently today if you knew that our present course as a Church and nation would end in the loss and destruction of our goods, our homes, our families and our nation? Are you willing to bet your children's future that it *won't* happen?

I'll be honest, I don't like being in jail. I don't like being away from my family. This is very difficult on my wife and my children. You too, may have to make sacrifices that are hard on your family. But if we refuse to make sacrifices in the name of "family", *we will end up sacrificing our families for generations.* Let me put it this way: where would America be if young men — many of them married — refused to go to war when our nation's freedom and survival was threatened? What if they said, "I just don't believe I should disrupt my family and career. I just bought a new home . . ." etc. We might be under a tyrannical regime flying a swastika.

Well, we *are* at war — for the lives of unborn children, the soul of our nation, and the future of our children. We, God's people, are going to *have to* make sacrifices and take extraordinary measures. At times it won't be "fun" for us or our families, but in the end it will be for our families and for the God of heaven. **And besides this, we will teach our children *by example* that there are things worth fighting for, worth dying for.** We will leave our children a *heritage of* *courage and commitment* to the Lord Jesus Christ and His Word. They will learn what is important in this life, and what is not; what is temporal and what is eternal. In the long run, our families will be the better for our sacrifices.

To the singles without children, I have one question: *where are you?* You are in a far easier place to make sacrifices than married men and women. What are you doing that is so important, that you couldn't take a year of two off, put your furniture, etc. in storage, and be the "Green Berets" of rescue and the pro-life movement? If you sat in jail for one week — or one year — or worked full-time with little or no pay for four months in the election of a pro-life candidate, is that really too great a sacrifice? Is whatever you're doing so important that you can't take a year or two off to work to stop this holocaust of children and perhaps rescue western civilization from a coming dark age? Remember folks, when Pearl Harbor was bombed, *everybody* stopped *everything*, and the *nation went to war*. If even a fraction of the Evangelical and Catholic community would get serious, *really serious*, about ending child-killing, even if it meant we suffered for a while, we could bring an end to this holocaust. God help us to rise to the occasion.

And what happens when we do suffer in this battle? *Suffering can be a great redemptive force.* "But the more they were oppressed, the more they multiplied and the more they spread abroad." (Exodus 1:12) Let's remember what happened in Atlanta in the summer of '88. The sacrifice and truly *minor* suffering of a few dozen incarcerated Christians helped sprout this movement around the nation. It's a Biblical principle, as we're standing for righteousness' sake, God will make those seeds of sacrifice sprout and multiply. If we can endure the hardships that God is calling us to, rather than run from them, I believe this movement will grow. If we don't, we may die.

So as a movement, we are at a critical time. The ultimate act of selfishness is to *take the life* of another human being for one's own convenience. The ultimate act of love is to *lay down one's life* for another human being. Those committed to child-killing have fully blossomed. Will we fully blossom in our holy calling to lay down our lives for the children? God help us to do so.

Yes, I could post an appeal bond and get out of jail. We could *all* post appeal bonds, but sooner or later, *we have to confront the enemy.* Sooner or later, *we have to pay our dues.* Sooner or later, *we have to fight.* The court system released this mass bloodshed, and now is the arch defender of child-killing. Tyrant judges and pro-death prosecutors (who smile and say "nice" things, "believe in God", and seem like "nice" people) will do all they can to protect child-killers and oppress and crush this movement. We can run, in which case they have been successful, or we can stand up to them, perhaps suffer, and ask God to use our stand to strengthen and encourage the body of Christ and to restore justice to this country.

Moms, dads, single people, grandparents, let me ask you a simple question. What are *you* willing to pay to see this holocaust ended and our nation reformed? At the close of the Declaration of Independence our founding fathers said, ". . . with a firm reliance on the Protection of Divine Providence, we mutually pledge to each other our Lives, our Fortunes and our Sacred Honor." It took that kind of commitment and sacrifice to give birth to this nation; it will take the same level of dedication and courage to reform her.

So what can you do? **Count the cost.** *Pray with fervency to overcome your own selfishness, apathy, or fear.* Then get your house in order and *fight*. Rescue as often as you can. Go to jail as often as you can. Get *seriously* (not superficially) involved in the political process in your community, lobbying and electing godly officials. Give no rest (in the First Amendment sense) to abortionists in your community; do the same to tyrant judges, prosecutors, and politicians who are attempting to hammer rescuers. Picket and sidewalk counsel as often as you can. Deliberately recruit new soldiers into this movement. Sacrifice financially — especially for those incarcerated in your community. Come up with some ideas of your own! Ask God to give you the grace to make any sacrifices He requires of you. . . .

In closing I want to challenge you to read this letter again and pray afresh about your part in this battle. I challenge you to read the book of Jeremiah before the Lord and see if your heart does not tremble within you for this country. Lastly, I believe God would challenge all of us to commit *our* lives, *our* fortunes, and *our* sacred honor — for the King and for the Reformation.

In His Service,
Randall A. Terry

* * * * *

October 15, 1989

An Open Letter to the Pastoral Community,

Greetings brothers, in the Name of Jesus, from the Fulton County Jail. . . . I've been praying for you and the Atlanta churches. I want to bare my heart to you in truth.

As you well know, our culture is degenerating into moral chaos at a frightening rate. I won't take time here to list the crises we face that could undo us as a civilization. Suffice to say, our gravest crime against humanity is the million and a half unborn children that are murdered every year in America. Twenty-five million mutilated bodies testify of our violent cruelty as a nation.

But I believe the moral crisis we face as a nation is a reflection of the crisis within the church — a crisis marked by the lack of courageous, sacrificial leadership.

Something terrible has happened in the Christian community. For two generations (at least) a poison has filled our collective soul. We've been soft. We've been complacent. We've been self-centered, self-serving, selfish saints, fighting to keep our own little world prosperous and undisturbed by unpleasantness; and we've done it all in the name of Jesus.

Tragically, this abounding selfish spirit is a reflection of the clerical community. (Please forgive my bluntness.) We've sought to build "respectable" ministries, forgetting that our Savior hung on a cross with all of its shame, and called us to follow in His steps. We're afraid to rock the boat, not realizing that the boat is sinking.

Let me put it simply. The clergy, with few notable exceptions, have miserably failed to lead the Church in Her call to be the "salt" and "light" of our culture. And America may soon testify from the ash-heap of history that we betrayed this holy calling.

I've been reading the book of Jeremiah lately. I beg you to do the same. What I've seen terrifies me. If the lessons of that book can be applied to this generation, we are in great danger.

The Israelites at the time were very religious. They went to worship at the temple. They offered sacrifices to God. They swore oaths in the Name of the Lord. But they were impure. Their "religion" had been polluted by the idolatry that surrounded them. And they wouldn't defend innocent children.

Jeremiah prophesied, "They have grown fat, they are sleek . . . they do not plead the cause of the fatherless; yet they prosper, and the right of the needy they do not defend. (Jer. 5:28)

Judah had degenerated into the abominable practice of child-sacrifice; offering their newborns in fire. (See Jer. 7:31, 19:5) Religious leaders who themselves did not participate in child-killing, nevertheless stood idly by (and prospered) while others murdered their children. God was outraged. And He ultimately destroyed the Temple, had foreign armies invade Jerusalem and burn it to the ground. Tens of thousands died by the sword, plague and famine; the few survivors were taken captive to Babylon.

Like Judah, we in the Church have become impure and idolatrous in our worship. For example, we've become acutely aware of humanism. We teach about it, rail against it, but are blinded to its towering presence in our midst. Many of our doctrines and emphases are nothing more than humanism baptized in a few Bible verses. At their core is the will of self, the love of self, and self-preservation. Oh yes, we have several well worn verses to justify our self-centered Christianity. But a tree is known by its fruit.

We are a generation of Christians that are materialistic — and greedy for more. We ignore the plight of the poor and needy; we shun inconvenience and flee from conflict; we know little or nothing of true sacrifice; suffering for the Gospel's sake seems strange to us; and we have ignored and perhaps despised Christ's mandate for us to pick up our cross daily, die to self, and follow Him.

Like Judah in Jeremiah's early days, we prosper, but we refused to protect the innocent children being slain in our nation. For the most part, we've stood idly by while millions of children have been brutally murdered in America's abortuaries. We ignore God's command to "rescue those unjustly sentenced to death." (Prov. 24:10-12, Ps. 82:1-4; Prov. 31:8-9; Is. 1:17) We are guilty of letting this holocaust rage on almost unabated.

Brethren, legalized child-killing simply could not exist in this nation without our continued complicity in this crime. Some of us lie to ourselves (or to our congregations) saying that stopping the killing of babies "isn't our calling" or it's a "social issue" or a "political issue"; but do we really believe that? Remember the Priest and the Levite who "passed by on the other side" while the man was dying in the ditch? Perhaps they told themselves they weren't called to a "ditch ministry", or they were too busy "preaching and serving the Lord" to help the man. Maybe they were afraid to get involved, but whatever their excuse, it just didn't wash. They were the goats, the failures of the story. They didn't love their neighbor.

And we, like them, have "passed by on the other side" while twenty-five million children died a brutal, untimely death in the "ditch" of America's abortion mills. Where were we? We have failed to love our neighbor. We have sinned grievously before Almighty God.

Our delusions have made us blind to the big picture. As the ever increasing cry of innocent blood ascends before God, crying for His vengeance, we inch closer and closer to destruction. Whether economic chaos, famine, drought, plagues, terrorism, a nuclear exchange, the collapse of our government, or any number of calamities of varying degree, God is going to avenge the blood of the innocent.

The question is, how severe will His judgement be? That, to a large extent, depends on us. Will we, by our actions give God a reason to remember mercy in the midst of Judgement? And lest we self-righteously think that "America deserves what she gets!" let's remember our children. If we do continue plummeting down this path, what horrors await our children and grand-children? Will we see them slowly starve to death before our eyes, or die from nuclear fallout? Or will they have to stand for truth and justice at the cost of their blood? Whatever happens, I fear we will be remembered with scorn and contempt — a disgrace to Church history — because in an hour when we could have turned the tide in America, we chose not to.

Now, the thought of cataclysmic judgement might seem overstated to some, ridiculous to others. And please understand, I am not talking about "Armageddon", "the end of the world", or the Lord's second coming. I'm talking about God judging America, the way that He has judged every civilization in history that turned its back on Him.

I ask you again, read the book of Jeremiah. He preached "coming destruction" for forty years, during some pretty prosperous times. People mocked. People laughed. Certain prophets and priests ridiculed his message saying, "God will not destroy us — we shall continue in peace and prosperity." and some of those same people died by the sword, plague, and famine — after they had cannibalized their own children.

Are we about the repeat this dreadful cycle of History? Are we going to continue on "business as usual"? Are we willing to risk our children's and grandchildren's future that God won't judge us? If He didn't spare Israel, His covenant nation, what makes us think He'll spare us?

So what do we do? Heed the cry of Jeremiah: Repent! Obey the demands of the prophet Isaiah: "Learn to do good; Seek justice; Rebuke the oppressor; Defend the fatherless; Plead for the widow." (Is. 1:17)

It's time to stop playing Church, and take the risky, sacrificial, financially draining, unrewarding, unpleasant, exciting, controversial, action necessary to end legalized child-killing in America. Action in the streets, action in the legislature. It's going to be a hard fight. Our enemies are entrenched, well financed, backed by the pro-abortion press, and freshly invigorated by the recent Webster case and some subsequent death victories. But we've got to fight. Everything is at stake. The survival of America is inextricably bound up in the fate of the children.

If we repent of our selfishness and apathy that has allowed child-killing to flourish, and restore justice for children, and dignity to mothers, we may survive. We will be judged for the blood already shed, but perhaps we will be spared some cataclysmic judgement. If we don't repent, we will perish. No nation can kill her offspring without God's judgement.

In closing, for those who think these are the words of a half crazed alarmist, let me ask you a question. In 1959, if someone had stood in an American pulpit and declared, "In 30 years we will have murdered 25 million children in the most barbaric ways imaginable; we will be killing handicapped newborns and unwanted elderly; prayer and Bible reading will be illegal in public schools; homosexuals will be marching in the streets; mayors in prominent cities will declare 'Gay Pride Week'; we will have a terrifying plague known as AIDS; Christian schools and home schools will be harassed by the government; Christianity will be mocked on TV sitcoms; Hollywood will produce a blasphemous movie, 'The Last Temptation . . .'; pornography — the debasing of women and children — will be rampant; children will be kidnapped and murdered in 'snuff' films; we will have government scandals beyond belief; hundreds of thousands of homeless; a cocaine crisis that is threatening the very security of our nation ; and school officials in New York State suggesting we teach third graders about condoms and anal sex." WHO WOULD HAVE BELIEVED IT?! Would not such a person be labeled an alarmist — a lunatic?

If we have plunged this far down the path of cruelty and moral anarchy in thirty years, where will we be thirty years from now? I shudder to think. God, please wake us up before it's too late.

Your fellow servant,
Randall A. Terry

APPENDIX B

MISSIONARIES TO THE PREBORN

They will proclaim His Righteousness,
to a people yet unborn — for He has done it.
Psalm 22:31

May the groans of the prisoners come before you;
by the strength of your arm preserve those condemned to die.
Psalm 79:11

"Missionaries to the preborn, in a spirit of obedience to God, come together to love our neighbors, including preborn children and their mothers and fathers, by intervening between them and the one who would kill the child and exploit the parents. Having no protection from the legal/judicial system, we, as Christians citizens, obligated by our consciences, which have been made conformable to the Scriptures, choose to identify by word and deed with their plight. We have resolved to pay the price of our convictions with humility and compassion toward our oppressors, keeping in mind the harmlessness of our Savior before His accusers and the defenselessness of the children before their executioners. If we are charged with crimes for loving our neighbor as ourselves, we will respectfully plead their case before the courts, and if imprisoned, we will minister as witnesses of God's love, compassion, and redemption to our fellow prisoners, offering the Word of Life through Jesus Christ our Lord."

With these words, Pastor Matt Trewhella, and fifteen Christians in Milwaukee, took the conceptual, spiritual, and practical step to make concrete the next phase of the pro-life movement. In their first brochure he described the cost in terms taken from Operation Rescue's 1989 call to return to Atlanta. "When God calls us to defend the innocent, He is simply calling us to do what He has always called us to, namely, *to be willing to give up our agendas and our goals to follow Him.* If God has given you a desire to rescue children continually, then you need to embrace what the prophet Isaiah said, 'For the Lord GOD helps me . . . therefore I have set my face like flint, and I know that I shall not be ashamed.' (50:7) The attack of the world is always that God is foolish for rescuing people by going to the Cross, by dying for them, and by throwing in His lot with those who are helpless and unwanted. It is time for us to do just that."

What is a Missionary to the Preborn?

Missionaries to the Preborn is the first Christian mission in America to target the preborn child as its people group. Being a missionary is more than a name change for activism. It reflects a whole dimension of the issue, which only the Church can speak to: the human need each child has for Jesus Christ and the obligation of the

Church to proclaim Him boldly in a way which ensures the child a chance to hear — what better way than to rescue his physical life as a tangible example of what Jesus Christ can do for his soul?

The missionary concept is simple, and as old as the Church itself: because not everyone can go to every mission field, the body of Christ sends those who are able to go to particular fields and stands behind them. We will now do this on behalf of the largest group of people in America who will never hear the Gospel — people in the wombs of mothers entering a death camp. And why not? Bringing the Good News to *all* mankind is the Church's proven vehicle to transform the world.

Their ministry is to those children whose mothers have avoided the crisis pregnancy centers, walked past the picketers, ignored the sidewalk counselors, and are entering the killing room. In a few moments those children will be dead. No legal recourse is available. They cannot protect themselves. By protecting them, missionaries remove the cooperation of the Church from their public murder and give a living demonstration of what Christ did on the Cross for us.

It is quite normal for ministries to children to result in the salvation of their parents. The experience of the missionaries is no exception. Countless mothers and fathers have accepted Christ as a result of the Good News being brought to their children.

Missionaries believe that it is worth bringing the Gospel to every child. And the Church is God's chosen vessel to bring the Gospel to "every creature under heaven."

Rescue daunts many either because they refuse to see the matter from the child's point of view, or because the potential penalties loom too great to justify the effort. Often this leads people to develop reasons why not only *they* must not Rescue, but why *no one else* should Rescue either. They see no middle ground between rescuing and not rescuing. The whole concept of missions breaks through this impasse, providing the middle ground for the whole Church, through the missionary, to walk into the death camp and end child-killing.

The heart of any mission must be a personal dedication to going as far as each member can to obey God. This is as true for those who support the missionaries as it is for the missionary himself. *The missionary who is rescuing will not succeed unless God moves in His people's hearts. Therefore, the plan is to rescue the unborn until enough of God's people outside of jail make it impossible to be arrested for living by the Gospel in their city. The missionaries have made no plans to succeed without God sending revival. God will bless only His Church. The question is not, "Is there a 'revival movement' going on?" but rather, "Knowing what I now know, am I revived? Does it take a mass movement for me to obey God and stand with His people?"*

About Prisoners Of Christ

Prisoners Of Christ is a ministry coordinated by Missionaries to the Preborn for both non-missionaries and missionaries who have been incarcerated for protecting children from death by abortion. By publishing a list of who is in jail, where the jail is, and which judge put them there, the missionaries give an opportunity for the Church to write letters, call civil authorities to accountability, and offer emergency financial help as needed (and it usually is).

The name "Prisoner Of Christ" has come to be a generic term for any pro-life prisoner. The term "P.O.C." used to refer to Prisoner Of Conscience. To the medical community at large, "P.O.C." is Product Of Conception, a term they use to strip human dignity from a helpless child. The pro-life prisoner is all of these.

Before changing its name in January of 1991 to *Missionaries to the Preborn*, the Atlanta missionaries called their fellowship *Prisoners Of Christ*. They sought to capture an important truth for all missionaries — and for that matter, for all Christians as well. A prisoner of Christ is someone who can say before God: "I am doing all I can to break with my covenant of cooperation with the death industry, and I am preparing myself, my family, and my church to take the necessary steps to break with it further in the coming years."

The Apostles seemed indifferent toward material possessions and suffering. Whether in want or plenty they would be content to obey God. They never clung to those things our lives and churches seem to revolve around today. Paul seemed to sum up his freedom — in or out of jail — when he called himself a Prisoner Of Christ — never a prisoner of Rome or Philippi. Often today Christians in jail are called "prisoners of conscience." We should respect the good intent of this title. For the Christian, however, it is the example of the Church through the ages which enlightens our conscience as it conforms to the Word of God which forms and binds it. Therefore, we want to point beyond what the world idealizes — the unfettered conscience — to what God blesses — the mind and heart transformed by obedience to His Word, rather than conformed to this world. If it were not for the Corinthians pushing him to prove himself, we would not have known how extensive Paul's willingness to suffer was. (I Corinthians 4:9-13; II Corinthians 4:7-18; 11:5-33) This is because he simply did not find either suffering or prosperity worth a great deal of comment. He was a prisoner of Christ, ordering his life so that he could obey God regardless of benefit or loss. For Paul, being a prisoner of Christ meant whether in jail, or out, he was always free because he was captive to the will of God.

Standing with a Missionary to the Preborn

When a Christian's obedience to God lands him in jail, it gives each of us a chance to multiply the impact of that witness by joining with him, whether or not we go to jail ourselves. Many of us have not arranged our lives so that we could go and physically do what the missionary did and so join him in jail. But it is still important for us to find ways to stand with him. Every way of joining such a witness is an important part of freeing ourselves, our affairs, our families, and churches for similar service to God, though perhaps in another field. We want to strive to be in a position where jail, beatings, or lawsuits are not the significant factor in the decisions we make about how and where we will obey God. It is only recently, and in America, that prison was not considered a live possibility for the faithful believer. The experience of missionaries and Rescuers is a return to what is far more normal in the experience of God's people through the centuries.

"Every part of the body working together" takes on a whole new dimension: how do we express our unity through the barrier of jails and man's rebellious "laws"? We begin by freeing ourselves to support those who have already left everything. Missionaries to the Preborn offers individuals, families, and groups the unique opportunity to share in the life of a full-time Rescuer by adopting a missionary. Your missionary's goal is to see each supporter taking as committed a stand in the things they do — both in support of the mission, as well as in the primary areas of their own calling in life — as your missionary does in the things he does.

By standing with your missionary financially and spiritually you make it possible for him to protect children more effectively. Your missionary, whether in jail or rescuing, has a powerful ministry to the judges, police, and child-killers who put him there — God, not man, is LORD. You amplify that message to the world as you hold authorities accountable for their oppression of Christians and the preborn by calling the authorities to bring them God's message: "Let My people go that they may serve Me."

If you decide to adopt and stand with a missionary to the preborn, tell your wife or husband, your children, and your in-laws. Particularly with your children share the sacrificial example of American Christians here on American soil. No longer is suffering for your faith some far-away Sunday school missionary story. Today, in America, Christians — just like those in your family — are in jail for their faith. And now your family is joining with them in their testimony.

Standing Spiritually with Your Missionary

☞ Put these concerns before a Sunday school class, prayer group, or church. Consider adopting a particular missionary, as a family, church, or any other group within a church.

☞ Set aside three times a day specifically for prayer, or one or more meals a week for prayer. Sleep on the floor one night a week and think of what a holding tank is like. Then think about how small your discomfort is — as well as the discomfort of your missionary — compared to that of an aborted child. Any time you wake up, pray for your missionary as well as members of the death squad.

☞ What is a death squad? It is those in a community who must cooperate in order for each child to be murdered: the abortionist, his staff, the arresting officers, the judges, those who run the jail, pastors in the community, the mothers. The missionaries will send you names of some of these key people. Pray for them!

☞ Pray that they would convert to true life-changing faith in Jesus Christ; and if not (for the committed killers and judges who protect them) pray the imprecatory Psalms as well. If any on the death squad are believers, pray that they will be bold, like Esther, to do what only they are in a position to do. Then pray that God will make you as bold as you are asking Him to make them.

☞ Pray for the regular inmates to whom your missionary ministers.

☞ Pray for the families of your missionary.

☞ Pray for God's blessing in every way on those who have committed themselves to this ministry in any way. Pray for those preparing to join this ministry at any level. Pray for all who continue the process of setting their houses in order to do all they can.

Standing Financially with Your Missionary

☞ Help support your adopted missionary. If he is married with children, their needs are the same as any family's, though they have probably trimmed them considerably.

☞ Suggest that your Sunday school, Bible study or prayer group financially support a rescuing missionary to the preborn and prisoners.

☞ Write him. Ask him to share stories of Rescue and prison ministry with your family and Church group. Missionaries tend to be quiet and rather undynamic in what they say. Their lives do the talking. People find most of them are normal unremarkable Christians who are determined to devote themselves to an amazing and remarkable God. What they have done is simply to refuse to say, "God, You just have to understand why I can't obey You in this area of life."

Standing Politically with Your Missionary

"Let My people go that they may serve Me!" Most people think of elections and campaigns. Missionaries think of the heart of true politics — encouraging people one on one to work together and stand unflinchingly for what is right. They reach out to those who protect abortion. They regularly and firmly encourage these protectors to turn from their coordinated protection of child-killing. If they will not, then they stand with the children at any cost, bringing them Good News, "Your executioner couldn't make it in today!" (Isaiah 52:7-10, 61:1-3) Every time your missionary is threatened with jail, is your opportunity to put forward the case for the preborn — the case for Christianity.

☎ Regularly, Regularly, Regularly, Regularly, Regularly. Once a day or once a week you will phone or write the judge who put your missionary in jail. This is not a short term flash-assault project. It is not a "project" at all. It is a witness of unflagging determination. The Christians return again and again and again to protect children by rescuing them, regardless of the jail sentences. More Christians mirror this commitment by calling judges again and again and again. We must break the short-range-fad disease which grips the Church. Over time, the impact grows. The world begins to realize that this is more than the excitable comfort-zone Christian they are used to dealing with. The force of normal everyday people who refuse to quit bears witness to a God in their midst Who will not quit. God has often used this sort of person — someone like you — to change the heart of a friend, a family, a church, or of a whole civilization.

☎   When you call or write, focus on two major issues:

1) Pleading for the protection of the children whose lives are in danger because the judge is holding Christians in jail who would otherwise be protecting those children.

2) Only Jesus Christ is the answer, so plead with them to let Him be Lord in their own lives, that they in their own daily work may live by His standards.

☞ **Your missionary in jail is *not* in need of help because he is stuck there.** *Getting out is easy enough, all he needs to do is cooperate with child-killers the way everyone else does.* He is in jail because the rest of our society is willing to work together to keep Christians from protecting the preborn, and he refuses to be reeducated and stop protecting them. He is in jail to give us all a chance to become a part of a solution that will last. He becomes your opportunity to bring heart change at the grass roots. Each phone call and letter adds weight to your and your missionary's refusal to cooperate with murder. Each contact with judge and jailer makes protecting children more socially acceptable and morally required. When we refuse to go along to get along, we are making a long-term change in Church and society possible. Each part of the Church has a different word for this — revival, reformation, awakening, reconstruction, renewal — but regardless of the vocabulary, it is the reign of Christ shown forth publicly in the lives of His people. It is that reign for which we all pray, work, and sacrifice.

Standing Physically with Your Missionary

Come and rescue children as often as you can. A missionary is strongly encouraged when he sees any Christian doing anything for the children, even if it is not in the city where he is being held. *This is far more important to him than any effort to get him out of jail.*

You do not need to throw your life away in order to rescue. You can become a short-term missionary. The larger mass Rescues of short-term missionaries legitimate the smaller daily Rescues of full-time missionaries, and the daily Rescues legitimate the mass Rescues.

The key to the short-term missionaries' rescuing strategy is that they try to save life and take as firm a stand against the child-killing system as they can. There are no minimum standards for Rescue. The children just want you to be there doing as much for them as you can. The missionary, on the other hand, has the freedom to take a firmer line. In fact, the Church has sent him out to take that firm line.

Philosophy

The missionary concept is a new step for the Church only in the pro-life arena. Historically it has been the Church's path from the beginning. Thus the primary fact about Missionaries to the Preborn is that it is a Gospel mission to the largest group of people in America who will never hear the Gospel — if the missionary cannot save their lives, they will be murdered within an hour of their first meeting. The best background material to understand their vision will not come from studying those who sought to bring social change through activism, but rather in the lives and biographies of great missionaries such as William Carey, C.T. Studd, Francis Xavier, Francis of Assisi, St. Augustine (of England), St. Patrick, St. Paul, and many others.

By applying the concepts of Christian missions, Missionaries to the Preborn focuses and modifies many things, which though present in activism and Rescue, were not made the central organizing themes:

☞ Missionaries are a small part of the body of Christ, deeply dependent on every part of the body performing its function faithfully. They are not crusading heroes here to straighten out the world — the Church must be the Church. They cannot replace the Church, only represent it. Missionaries are committed to a local Church in their field between jail time, and they function in it as much as they are able to. They enable the Church to be represented through them. They do not reduce the Church to an activist pool for social agendas of reform. They are committed to the same long-term agenda as the Church is — our God reigns — and they avoid short-term hype.

☞ A missionary is someone who has, as much as possible, freed himself of all worldly cares to devote full-time to rescuing the children whenever he is free of jail. Those who become missionaries have accepted a call to become a martyr for their witness to the Truth in the arena to which God has called them to lay down their lives. Thus when they are released from trials and prison, they are released to continue bringing good news to the preborn. In a word, whenever they are released from jail they are released to rescue.

☞ Being a missionary is a full-time job. Whether it is Rescuing, or sidewalk counseling, or some other task, the key is that a missionary must be primarily a self-starter and a doer directly engaging the killers and mothers personally. They are not organization heads or organizers. Their "ministry" is not too important to risk going to jail. They have tried to strip down every organizational function to a minimum and give it to someone who is not called to the full-time work of intervention. They do not want anything by which the world could hold them hostage, whether it is their possessions, jobs, the charges, lawsuits, jail time, or the threat of losing their organizations and political/media clout. They simply Rescue as often as they are out of jail, whether alone or in groups ranging from two people to ten thousand.

☞ They are missionaries to the *preborn*. Everyone else is secondary. Once they make anyone else primary or equal to the child, then sitting in front of the door becomes moot. But if they block the door for the *child*, then even if the mother curses at them the entire time they are getting arrested (which is rare), and goes in and turns her baby over to the hired killers, what they did was not in vain — they loved the *child*. If they slip into the mindset of "I'm trying to stop wickedness," they will become overwhelmed. Why? Because wickedness will continue. But when they do what they do to love their neighbor, they can live with whatever happens to them. It is not frustrating to sit in jail for loving your neighbor, because it is done — you have loved the child. But if you are trying to stop wickedness in general, it will continue, and your sitting in jail can seem pointless.

☞ *Their actions in custody are designed to make plain the two great facts of their incarceration*: The missionary would be saving children's lives if it were not for 1) a legal system determined to hold him in jail, and 2) a Church which allows the legal system to hold him.

☞ Missionaries focus on their particular city, perhaps even a single abortion clinic within that city. They do not shift their focus, and they rescue whenever free. Thus they have changed some of the tactics which have come to be associated with Rescue. *One such former tactic was that of refusing to cooperate throughout the system*. Instead, missionaries cooperate in custody because they want to make the single focus of their work the fact that they would rescue whenever free if it were not for the dedication of the city to hold them in jail, and the willingness of the Church to tolerate their imprisonment. *Another former tactic was that of expressing solidarity with each other by withholding names*. Instead, missionaries express solidarity by rescuing whenever free. If a fellow missionary is held longer on higher or extra charges, they join him in solidarity by continuing to rescue, not by other means. *A third former tactic was that of never posting bond or paying a fine*. Because their vision is long-term, missionaries normally will not post bonds; but they might post a bond if an unforeseen circumstance arises. When it is dealt with, rather than wait for their trial date, they will return and rescue even if it means being put back in jail.

☞ For those who support them, missionaries create a rich field of opportunity to enter into the battle for the preborn at many levels. If the system decides to use prison as its major weapon, then those who support them can call to accountability every level of public officials in the city for their jailing of innocent people. Those who call say, *"Let My people go that they may serve Me!"* Or, if the legal system decides *not* to throw Christians into jail, then the missionary has lowered the cost for the part-time missionary, providing a field for more people to rescue with greater freedom from legal persecution.

☞ The missionary's job is not to battle the system, but to protect children as often as possible. He refuses to let court dates and preparation get in the way of the next Rescue. The battle with the system is the job of those who have adopted the missionary and stand with him. It is only made necessary when judges and policemen play politics and crusade for child-killing on demand by imposing harsh sentences. The missionary is a realist when it comes to the laws of men and their enforcers. He expects neither victory nor mercy in court; It is his opportunity to bear witness to Jesus Christ and His little ones.

History

When Operation Rescue was first launched in 1988, most of us signed up envisioning tens of thousands of Rescuers in every city, and hundreds of thousands at national events. Though it means many different things to different people, the single word for this is "win" — we thought we could *win*. We risked everything, thinking that we would not have to lose everything in order to *win*, or that when we *won* we could get it all back. But what is *winning*? Is it getting in and out of jail successfully? Is it saving a life? Is it ridding a city of child-killing, or getting laws changed? Is it being willing to obey God though none of these things happen? It can be all of these things and more, because these are all elements of a transformed society — or if that is too big a concept, of transformed lives. In 1988 getting people to accept the idea of Rescue itself was radical. But we found it would take more to make child-killing impossible and unthinkable. Will we step up to the plate?

In the summer of 1989, Operation Rescue was peaking. If we could not make this peak the basis of the next step, then we would slump and all those who had joined the effort for the quick *win* would be shaken out. Was there still reason to rescue? What is our price? Did we repent or not? Will I throw in my lot with the unwanted, and boldly yet humbly declare, *"If you reject them you reject me"*?

Each Christian comes to his own conclusion. The conclusion of the missionaries is that a social movement to transform society is both possible and necessary, but that it will not be built — that is to say, we will not be able to *win* — apart from a core of those willing to risk everything for Jesus Christ, and to spend a considerable piece of their lives in the process. Real transformation of society will only come when the transformers are themselves transformed. We believe that God will move, but He will found that move on the faithfulness of His people, not by waving an exciting cost-free wand. Our experience in the 1988 Siege of Atlanta, as well as the Summer of Mercy Rescues in Wichita in 1991, has borne this out — unity within the pro-life movement, a taste of revival, strong pastoral leadership and involvement, even political support from the mayor of Wichita, the governor of Kansas, and the U.S. Attorney General's office, is no substitute for a Church which is willing to die. It is this focus which the Missionaries will provide in the years to come. We may never get another opportunity like Atlanta or Wichita. But if we do, will we walk through the door? In order to *win* tomorrow — whenever that tomorrow comes — we must begin today to lay the foundation for that battle and for those who will fight it.

In the fall of 1989, Operation Rescue gave a national call to come to Atlanta to die in order to *win*. We gambled on there being enough people willing to leave everything; that the group of Rescuers in Atlanta would slowly grow; that in time, the city would be dealing with 150 or more people who were incorrigibly Christian, whose example would match their rhetoric and would ignite the rest of the Christian community. By February it was felt that Atlanta was too big — surely there was some city somewhere where the price would be lower. Most left, but some of us remained in Atlanta and began developing many of the ideas you have read about in this book.

In the spring and summer of 1990, Pastor Matt Trewhella of Milwaukee, instead of coming to Atlanta as he had originally planned, was putting together a similar full-time Rescue effort in Milwaukee. He was struck by the similarity between full-time Rescue and Missions. He went to Earl Parvin's *Missions U.S.A.*, the premier book on missions in America. After studying every mission he realized that there are over 400 Christian missions in America and not one of them has targeted the preborn child as its people group. I was serving five months in jail in Atlanta at the time and was on the phone with him regularly. As I heard him develop the concept of missions, I saw the things we were articulating in Atlanta fall into place.

On September 1, 1990, in Milwaukee, Wisconsin, 15 people led by pastor Matt Trewhella took the example and ideas of the Rescuers in Atlanta and welded them into a single coherent concept: *Missionaries to the Preborn*. This was more than just a name change for pro-life activism. It opened a door for the Church to find its historic place of ministry in this matter — every child has a deep need for Jesus Christ, and the Church has an obligation to proclaim Him boldly in a way that enables the child in the womb to live to hear the Good News.

As with every other pioneering mission, where there is no willingness to risk losing everything, the mission will fly apart at the seams. Atlanta had heard the rhetoric before. There was no reason for either the legal system or the Church to think that we would be any different from the past. So the city assumed we would pay fines and leave like everyone else; but we did not. When the city of Milwaukee saw the missionaries' resolve, it decided not to imitate Atlanta. Therefore, Milwaukee has for the most part kept its courts and jails out of the middle of the dispute between Christians and child-killers. The history in Atlanta is one of prison with brief glimpses of the outside world, and then rescue with little Church support. The story of Milwaukee, by contrast, has been one of a grueling daily presence focused on one abortion clinic, keeping it shut down for a year before it finally closed. The risk is not lower in Milwaukee, because every day they continue to rescue could be their last for a long time. This threat keeps many groups from even trying to rescue daily in other cities. Though they want what the Milwaukee missionaries have, they do not want to risk what they risk.

In Atlanta, the Missionaries were originally called *Prisoners of Christ* because of the time they spend in jail. In January of 1991 they changed their name to *Missionaries to the Preborn*. The average Atlanta Rescuer spends 9 months of the year in jail. Their spiritual presence is a reminder to all missionary cities that when a missionary says, "We will rescue at any cost to ourselves," it is more than just rhetoric. But what is more, in Atlanta, thanks to one of their early members who now sidewalk counsels, over 950 children have been confirmed saved from abortion. Most of these were not saved through Rescues; but the Rescuers' fasting and prayer while in jail, and their tactical fearlessness, matched by the courage of the sidewalk counselors, have caused Atlanta police officers to back off of the counselors, and have broken the spiritual authorities in those death camps, giving the sidewalk counselors tremendous freedom and authority.

In Milwaukee, the missionaries were prepared for the same sort of jail time, but the city decided not to waste its resources imprisoning the unimprisonable. So in Milwaukee, they have remained free to rescue every day the death camp they targeted was open. In September of 1991, one year later, Bread and Roses folded and Dr. Jakobowski, the abortionist, left town for good. Many child-killers have quit killing in that city as well, leaving only six who grimly hang on.

Milwaukee's missionaries are perhaps best known for stopping the killer, Jakobowski, at a freeway rest stop and keeping him from getting to his death camp until late afternoon. It took five hours for 53 police officers in two different states, police dogs, a helicopter, and 15 squad cars, to get the killer to Milwaukee, where he was able to kill only one child. (Do you realize how much muscle our abortion culture is willing to put into ripping each child from the womb?)

Much more could be said, but these are the crucial ideas and events which anyone who wishes to support or start a similar group in their city must keep crystal clear. Many people are attracted by the freedom to rescue with impunity in Milwaukee and the powerful effectiveness of the sidewalk counseling in Atlanta. They very much want those things for their city, but often they shy away from the utter fearlessness (linked with lonely, thankless hours in the dark) of those who are at the heart of each effort. They wish that the fruit of this effort could be imitated without the cost of its daily risk. The Atlanta missionaries are a sober reminder of the level of commitment each missionary must have if he is to persevere under any circumstances.

**If you want to know more about this ministry,
don't hesitate to get in touch with us.
Three of our field offices are listed on the next page.**

MISSIONARIES TO THE PREBORN: FIELD OFFICES

Missionaries to the Preborn is a fellowship of full-time Rescuers dedicated to a specific mission field. They now operate in Atlanta, Milwaukee, and Wichita. There are 45 missionaries as of this printing.

If you want to adopt a missionary, or become a regular supporter of the fellowship as a whole, or begin a missionary fellowship in your city, you can get in touch with *Missionaries to the Preborn* at their field addresses:

ATLANTA: (404) 439-1240
                                1033 Franklin Rd. # 297
                                Marietta, GA   30067

MILWAUKEE: (414) 536-1038
                                P. O. Box 25204
                                Milwaukee, WI   53227

WICHITA: (316) 794-3362
                                  P. O. Box 20915
                                Wichita, KS   67208